How to Plan an Elegant Second Wedding

How to Plan an
ELEGANT
Second Wedding

Achieving the Wedding You Want
with Grace and Style

Julie Weingarden Dubin

THREE RIVERS PRESS • NEW YORK

Published in the United States by Three Rivers Press, an imprint of the Crown Publishing Group, a division of Random House, Inc., New York.
www.crownpublishing.com

THREE RIVERS PRESS and the Tugboat design are registered trademarks of Random House, Inc.

Originally published in the United States by Prima Publishing, a division of Random House, Inc., Roseville, California, in 2002.

Interior illustrations by Kate Vasseur.

Library of Congress Cataloging-in-Publication Data
Dubin, Julie Weingarden.
    How to plan an elegant second wedding : achieving the wedding you want with grace and style / Julie Weingarden Dubin
        p.   cm.
    Includes index.
    1. Weddings—Planning. 2. Remarriage. I. Title.
HQ745.D83   2002
395.2'2—dc21   2002029029

ISBN 0-7615-1500-3

10 9 8 7 6 5 4 3

Printed in the United States of America

First Edition

To Bobby and Joshua, second chances,
and dreams coming true.

Contents

Acknowledgments

Some guys think "wedding talk" ends after the engagement. But my guy knows better. Bobby, thank you for your patience and love in dealing with a wife with "weddings on the brain." You are the most incredible husband, father, and friend, and I'm grateful for every day we have together.

Joshua, your smile lights up my world. Thank you for all of your hugs and kisses of encouragement. You are truly the greatest gift daddy and I could have asked for.

Mom and Dad, thank you for your love and for making a difference. Mom, your talents as a mother, grandmother, friend, wife, and writer amaze me. Thank you for everything you've taught me. Dad, I'm the luckiest girl in the world to have you as my father. You continue to inspire me. You knew I could do it and you always help me see the big picture. Thank you for believing in me and for motivating me.

Thank you Kevin and Shelley for your love and friendship. I'm so lucky to have you both in my corner. Thank you Gama Peggy and Nana Sylvia for your love, support, and wisdom.

Thank you Sheila, Howard, and Carole for being such caring and thoughtful parents and grandparents. Thank you Susan, Michael, Brandon, Dylan, David, Jeffrey, and Beth for your laughter and love. Thank you to my wonderful aunts, uncles, and cousins, who have always been, and will always be, an important part of my life. I'm so fortunate to have such a caring family.

Thank you Lisa, Danny, and Charlie for your support and for allowing my guys to hang with you every weekend while I was immersed in this project.

Thank you Angie for encouraging me to write this book.

Thank you to my friends and my dear bridesmaids, some of whom didn't mind getting all dressed up for me twice in a lifetime.

Thank you Jacquie for caring so wonderfully for Joshy. Your helping hand will always be appreciated.

I thank my awesome neighbors for always checking in, rooting for me, and on many occasions, feeding my family!

Thank you to the amazing team at Prima Publishing. It's been a privilege to work with you. Denise Sternad, you are an editor with vision and I love working with you. Thank you for being open to my ideas. Michelle McCormack, thank you for your superb talents in shaping my manuscript and for appreciating the author's voice. Jennifer Dougherty Hart, thank you for your enthusiasm toward this project and for believing in it enough to see that our publicity "wish list" becomes a reality!

Thank you to the countless second-time brides and grooms, experts, and vendors who shared their stories and knowledge for this book. I truly appreciate your time, interest, and excitement in seeing that second-time couples have the information they need to plan the wedding of their dreams.

Thank you fellow Prima Publishing author Sharon Naylor for your support, and thank you Ellen Cogen for your wonderful legal guidance.

Thank you Denise Schipani and Diane Forden for giving me the opportunity to first open up about being a second-time bride in the pages of *Bridal Guide* magazine.

Thank you to my many wonderful magazine editors who allow me to constantly learn and grow as a writer.

Thank you to the American Society of Journalists and Authors—a group of dedicated, helpful, and talented writers who I'm proud to call my colleagues.

Introduction

So it's true? You're in love and getting married! Congratulations! Welcome to the second-time sisterhood, a group that's growing by the minute.

Because it's been a few years since you were in planning mode, this book will walk you through the wedding prep steps and let you know which rituals aren't necessary the second time around. You'll also learn that you have endless options in planning an elegant second wedding. You can make this wedding much more personalized than your first.

Your first wedding probably was pretty much your mother's wedding. She took control and guided you through the wedding-vendor maze. But don't fear that you're in it alone this time. Your groom is likely to be very much involved in the planning—a concept that is quite foreign to first-time brides. If you have children, they may want to help. And then, of course, you have me.

With This Book—A Friend and a Guide

I'm guessing you already bought some bridal magazines because you want to see all the new bridal fashions. You probably also will research wedding vendors on the Web. What you may find along the way is that the magazines and Web sites might not address your needs as a second-timer, at least not in the depth you'd like.

You may have already found that the first-time-bride books don't apply to you. There is so much information you don't need. You don't need a 300-step time line of what must be done between months six and seven of your engagement. You may not even have six months in your engagement. You know how to hire a florist and a caterer—you've entertained before. You want answers to questions that are unique to second-time brides, from the roles your children can play to whether or not to ask your fiancé to sign a prenup.

I've talked to many second-time brides who feel they are left out of the mix when it comes to wedding planning information. "For a first wedding there are a number of books and magazines that cover everything you need to know," says Becky, who got married for the first time at age 26 and the second time at age 30. "For a second wedding, nothing exists, so you just have to go on instinct. I didn't know if it was 'proper' to wear white, get married in a church, have bridesmaids or a wedding ceremony."

In chapter 1, I tell my "second wedding" story and provide a list of what you *can* do for your second wedding. In chapter 2, you'll learn how to manage mixed emotions (if you have any) and how not to care about what people think. If you're a widow, you'll learn about how to deal with feelings unique to your situation. Chapter 3 delves into the fun of picking a type of wedding and time of year. You get to decide if you want to do a chic city bistro get-together or a small seaside wedding. Chapter 4 tackles the fun topic of money and who pays in a second wedding, and chapter 5 helps with the guest list.

Chapter 6 gives you a refresher course on booking the big five: the place, music, clergy, photographer, and florist. You'll learn what important questions to ask as well as how to deal with vendor attitude. In chapter 7, we get the paper pushing over with, from necessary divorce documents to prenuptial agreements. Chapter 8 explains how to personalize your ceremony, and chapter 9 allows the groom to have his say. In chapter 10 you'll choose among brunch, buffet, or a seated dinner, and you'll learn what questions to ask the caterer. In chapter 11 you get to set the mood and decide how to bring your vision to life with the décor.

Chapter 12 gives you the scoop on photos, video, and entertainment, and whether or not to have toasts. Chapter 13 helps you decide what to wear. Chapter 14 answers your registering questions, and Chapter 15 gives you transportation options. Chapter 16 explores invitations, from style to wording, and chapter 17 lets you get creative with your vows, Web site, and programs. You get gorgeous in chapter 18 (and learn that you do not have to diet!). In chapter 19 we talk about friends and their roles in the wedding, and chapter 20 explains how your children can be involved not only in your wedding but throughout your engagement. Chapter 21 covers rehearsals and what essentials to carry in your bag. It also offers tips for second-marriage success from happily married second-timers.

Wow, that was a lot! And there is much more inside. As we go along, you'll find that everything centers around these three beliefs:

1. Every wedding is a celebration. It doesn't matter how many times you've worn a fancy white dress. This is the first time you and your groom are marrying each other!

2. There are no rules. Besides, if you're divorced, you're not going to get hung up on some ancient etiquette. After all, you've already broken the rules.

3. Second chances are sweet.

Why You Need to Recall Your First Wedding

You're likely to look back on your first wedding, and that's okay. That was the only other time you were a bride. But the beauty of your situation is that you can take advantage of your been-there-done-that knowledge. You know you can handle having all eyes on you as you walk down the aisle. You know whether having the makeup person show up five hours before the ceremony is key for you. You know if you wasted too much time making rounds to the tables and didn't spend enough time dancing. When you consider the kind of wedding you want, there is good in being a second-time bride. You may have gone through hard times to get to where you are today, but there is something to be said for what you've learned.

Many of the psychologists I interviewed say it's wise to draw from experience. But that doesn't mean you have to get stuck in the past or try to resurrect your past relationship. You get to do things differently. You can make your wedding unique to your current relationship.

My husband, Bobby, proposed in the middle of the afternoon on a Caribbean beach. I thought he was joking. But as he leaned over his lounge chair, he assured me that one knee was in the sand. I guess I believed him, because I ended up scooping up some sand and saving it. Before I knew it we were making regular long-distance calls to my mother so she could start working the phones to line up the location and officiant.

In less than six months, we were married in a gorgeous ballroom at a charming historic hotel. Our black-tie affair for 120 guests featured a sit-down dinner, open bar, live band, and magnificent flowers. I suppose etiquette ladies of yesteryear would frown upon such nonquiet merrymaking, but this isn't their book.

In the same spirit, this isn't their wedding, or your mother's, your in-laws', or your friends'. It's yours. And if you want to have a grand celebration, by all means, *do!*

You are ready and eager to get married. With a little support from this book and me, you'll enjoy the planning process. This may not be your first wedding, but this is your first wedding to each other. And what a wonderful wedding it will be. Let the fun begin!

How to Plan an Elegant Second Wedding

Speaking from Experience

WHY I WROTE THIS BOOK

I'm a second-time bride with two elegant weddings under my belt—or should I say bustle? Research and personal experience prepared me for wedding planning, and my journalism background led me to top experts. I write articles for national magazines covering everything from relationships, parenting, and psychology to business, pop culture, and health, and I have to say, I combined all of my areas of interest in researching and writing this book.

I want you to know that you're not alone. Remarriage is common. The Stepfamily Association of America, Inc., estimates that about 46 percent of all marriages are remarriages for at least one of the people involved. It also estimates that roughly 75 percent of divorced persons eventually remarry, and about 65 percent of remarriages involve children from a prior marriage, forming stepfamilies. Men and women opened up to me about their innermost feelings, from their worries about becoming a stepparent to their decisions on how to spend their wedding budget.

Not only are Americans remarrying; we aren't wasting much time. According to the Association of Bridal Consultants, roughly four years will pass before one remarries after a divorce.

Couples planning second weddings want resources. In addition to sharing my personal wedding-planning experience, I also share the stories of second-time brides and grooms around the country and the unique weddings they planned. There is also advice from national experts, including the usual suspects (photographers, florists, and wedding coordinators), the fun folks (celebrity party planners and dress designers), the necessary folks (financial planners and lawyers), and the bonus bunch (national bridal magazine editors, relationship experts, and psychologists).

One thing I didn't have to ask anyone is what it's like being a second-time bride. I *know* what it's like. I know the thrill of finding love again. I know about the mixed emotions and sometimes even guilt that can come with being a second-time bride. I know what it's like to answer to three different last names. I know what it's like to pay vendors with your own money. I know what it's like to accept money from your parents—again. I know what it's like to shop for attire for wedding number two. But mostly, I know what it's like to be confused and wonder where to turn for advice on planning a second wedding.

When I got engaged, there was little information available on second weddings, and even less offering modern options. Much of the information I found was for older women. At 31, I felt young enough to wear a dress—not a "cocktail suit." Where were the articles that could guide me?

I learned that there are many young second-time brides today. Beth Reed Ramirez, editor of *Bride Again* (www.brideagain.com), an online magazine for women planning to remarry, says although the magazine's average reader is 39, many readers are in their twenties.

According to the National Center for Health Statistics, younger women who divorce are more likely to remarry. Data from the

1995 National Survey of Family Growth shows that 81 percent of women divorced before age 25 remarry within 10 years, and 68 percent of divorced women older than age 25 remarry within 10 years.

I'm thrilled that brides like you are celebrating your second weddings in style and aren't letting outdated etiquette rules make you think you have to sneak off and quietly get married with no fanfare. Should you get a touch of the engagement blues because naysayers question your decision to have a wedding, remember these two words: *You can.*

You can have a beautiful ceremony.
You can have a religious ceremony.
You can have a church, temple, or synagogue wedding.
You can wear a wedding gown.
You can wear white.
You can wear a veil.
You can have bridesmaids and groomsmen.
You can have your children in your wedding.
You can have a large wedding.
You can have a wedding cake.
You can register.
You can have showers.
You can have a beautiful and elegant second wedding.

Second-Time Acceptance

GETTING OVER YOUR SECOND-WEDDING GUILT

Chances are, you're ecstatic about your wedding. After one marriage, you've finally found the real one, and hopefully you'll think of this as saving the best for last. And if you do, feel free to skip right to chapter 3. But just in case you do have some emotional concerns, this chapter discusses some very common thoughts and fears experienced by second-time brides. Read on to put your mind at ease—you should not start planning this wedding until you're ready to do so in the form of pure bliss!

There are plenty of wedding books out there that cover everything from picking diamonds to daisies, but many women I've interviewed were at a loss when it came to finding information on dealing with the emotions of being a second-time bride. They can handle booking a florist and lining up the perfect caterer. After all, many of them are pros who broker deals all day long, whether it is with a major company or a fussy five-year-old. But they're not sure what to do about upsetting emotions that may hit at what is supposed to be a happy time.

If you have any doubts, I'll bet they are not about whether or not you are marrying the right person. It may be that you doubt yourself as you embark on another wedding and marriage. Relax, this isn't a character flaw. Just acknowledge your feelings, and while you're at it, try to be good to yourself.

Managing Mixed Emotions

Second-time brides have more to contend with than calling the girls to spread the news about the engagement. No matter how excited you are about your upcoming marriage, you still may be grappling with some unsettling feelings about being a bride again. Is this wedding going to bring up memories of your first wedding and thoughts about your first marriage? Maybe you're wondering how you are going to tell your children and ex-husband. When you look at your children from your previous marriage, are you going to wonder if they are thinking, "Why is Mommy marrying someone else—someone other than Daddy?"

You wonder whether you can have a traditional wedding and whether or not you should elope. If you have a second wedding and want to invite the same guests who helped you celebrate your first wedding, will you feel embarrassed when they see you walk down the aisle again? Will you feel funny accepting gifts? I know I did.

Two-hundred-plus friends and relatives saw me walk down the long synagogue aisle the first time. I wore a beautiful ecru-colored princess gown complete with the appropriate wardrobe attachments—crinoline, veil, bustier. Mom and Dad met me halfway down the aisle, and I exchanged vows with my first husband on the bimah (platform in a synagogue) of the synagogue that I had belonged to since birth.

My parents were extremely supportive throughout my divorce. Even though they liked my first husband, I'm their daughter. Forever. No matter what. They were such troupers, always there with a listening ear when I'd call home long-distance, crying about the fact that I had just spent my lunch hour in a lawyer's office discussing assets, and later, when I'd lament that I might not ever meet someone and fall in love again.

I felt that I brought shame to my parents because all of their friends witnessed our union, our wedding was announced in the community, and then two years later it ended. I'm sure it must have been a bit embarrassing for my parents, but they just told me they wanted me to be happy.

Divorce hits roughly half of all marriages, but not in the world where I grew up. My parents have been happily married for more than 35 years, and their parents were married until my grandfathers passed away. My parents' circle of friends all stayed married. My getting a divorce was quite radical.

No one said anything to me that was judgmental. I just felt funny when it came time to go through the motions of planning another wedding. Did I deserve another party when my family and friends all helped me celebrate my first wedding in full force, giving me their blessings and gifts? Then I started imagining ridiculous scenarios. What if people snickered as I walked down the aisle? Would they talk about which gown they liked better?

I found strength in the belief that my nearest and dearest family members and friends were happy for me and eager to help me celebrate. It also helped that I met several times with the rabbi who was marrying us. I expressed my concerns to him, and he told me not to worry. He said that every wedding is a reason for celebration. And I knew he could relate. He's a second-time groom.

Mixed emotions are natural. The good news is that the mixed emotions can serve as a good motivator to begin premarital

My Panel of Experts

• Judith Coche, Ph.D., clinical associate professor of psychology in psychiatry at the hospital of the University of Pennsylvania; senior clinical associate, department of clinical psychology at the University of Pennsylvania; and owner of The Coche Center in Philadelphia.

• Drs. Les and Leslie Parrott, authors of *Saving Your Second Marriage Before It Starts* (Zondervan/HarperCollins) and founders of the Center for Relationship Development at Seattle Pacific University.

• Judith Sills, Ph.D., clinical psychologist based in Philadelphia and contributing editor on marriage for *Family Circle* magazine.

• Roberta Temes, Ph.D., a New York City psychotherapist and clinical assistant professor, psychiatry, at SUNY Health Science Center.

• Ann Rosen Spector, Ph.D., a clinical psychologist in Philadelphia and an adjunct member of the department of psychology at Rutgers University in Camden, New Jersey.

education. You can explore your feelings by talking to a counselor, or you can sort through your feelings by keeping a journal. Just letting your thoughts spill onto the pages without having to worry about what you are saying can be a great mental release.

It's likely that a big cause of your mixed emotions is the painful emotional residue lingering from your first marriage or first wedding. Judith Coche, Ph.D., says that's to be expected. "A divorce or death dampens the thrill of the first marriage and carries baggage into the second," she notes.

Even if your first wedding was a blast, your ex was a doll, and things ended amicably, you may still wonder why the marriage didn't work. According to Drs. Les and Leslie Parrott, a second marriage presumes a failure of the first one even if you weren't the one who decided to call it quits.

If you are divorced you may find yourself asking if your second marriage can sustain the test of time. You are normal if you worry that your second marriage might fail, says Judith Sills, Ph.D. "There is this romantic myth that you will know when someone is the one and when it's forever, and we think everyone feels this," she says. "Second-time brides feel doubt because they have lived long enough to challenge the myth."

But the good news is that time has passed, wounds have healed, and you have learned what you need and what you won't settle for. Now you can look forward to a future with a strong, healthy marriage.

Wedding Day Reflections

I had mixed emotions at first, but then I thought, *this is the first time my fiancé and I are marrying each other, so why not celebrate big?* We wanted to share the moment with our family and friends.

—Carolyn

CHRISTINE'S STORY

I got married the first time at age 26 and I was 29 at my second wedding. I had concerns about wearing a white dress again and about receiving gifts, but my feelings of embarrassment went deeper than that. I'm half Japanese, and in Japanese families, the one thing you don't do is get divorced. It literally brings shame to your family. I was so entrenched in thinking, "Did I deserve a wedding? Did I deserve gifts?" Most of my worry came from my own concerns about propriety. I think I got a lot of my values from the Victorian literature I read growing up. After I got divorced, I thought no one else would ever want me again. That was not the case! I eventually learned to accept that just because I was in a failed marriage once doesn't mean my next marriage would fail. I am such a different person than I was the first time I got married. Does that mean that my second marriage won't end in divorce? No. But I am so much more confident and openly committed to making the marriage work, and I know my husband is too.

MISSY'S STORY

When I got married the first time I was 23, and in a way I think I was just following the natural pattern of what I saw around me. Maybe it's a Southern cultural thing, but where I grew up, "good" girls go to college, meet a guy, and get married. I'm now 33 and I'm about to get married to a wonderful man. Even though I've made a more mature decision this time, and I feel confident about it, I still feel guilt in marrying for a second time. There is still a certain stigma that surrounds divorce, even in this day and age where it has become much more prevalent. I have openly discussed my feelings of guilt with my fiancé, family, and friends. I think that has been the best remedy. There will always be skeptics in the world who view your divorce and your second marriage in a negative light ("How is she going to make this one work when she couldn't make the first one work?") but you can't let it bother you.

Second-Time Smarts

Sure, you've gained wisdom and maturity, but premarital counseling may give you that extra boost of confidence before you walk down the aisle. To find a psychologist in your area, call the American Psychological Association at 800-964-2000.

When You're a Widow—Coping with the Guilt of Leaving Your First Husband Behind

If you are a widow, you may feel guilt about moving on and leaving your first husband and his family behind. Even if you are still close to his family, you may wonder if exchanging vows with someone else will hurt them. You may worry that you are hurting your children—that they won't understand how you can forget Daddy and marry another man.

Lisa Iannucci, founder of www.young widowsandwidowers.com, a Web site that offers support for widows and widowers, says that young widows have several concerns when it comes to remarrying:

- How will their children adjust to being in a blended family?
- How will their first husband's family take the news?
- Has enough time passed since their first husband's death that they feel ready to get married again?
- How will they cope if they have to go through the same kind of devastating loss again?

Professionally Speaking

Don't be surprised if planning a second wedding makes you reminisce about your first one, and you uncover grief you did not expect. If you are concerned about reliving too many memories with a similar style wedding, plan something totally different.

—Lisa Iannucci, founder of www.youngwidowsand widowers.com

MICHELE'S STORY

I was 23 years old at my first wedding and 32 at my second wedding. I felt absolutely guilty about moving on and leaving my first husband behind. My first husband died of cancer, and as my second wedding got closer, my feelings of guilt and sadness about moving on were pretty tangible. I was very sad. I wanted a very small ceremony so that my first husband's family wouldn't have to be there to see me get married again. I didn't want to have to worry about what they were thinking or feeling. I am still close with his family and I invited them to the reception because I still wanted them to be a part of it. During the ceremony the day was overcast, and then all

Learning to Love Again

Judith Coche, Ph.D., shares her expert advice and personal experience as a widow who found love again:

• "Live for today. At my second wedding, my husband and I gave our guests mugs with the phrase, 'Our greatest gift is the time we share.' Every morning we drink our coffee with these mugs as a reminder of how precious our time is together. Loss of a beloved husband can sweeten finding another partner to love. It is like being doubly blessed."

• "Remember the past. It is not necessary to leave your first husband behind. He remains with you in your heart for every day of your life, even as you recoup. You don't need to leave his family behind. My matron of honor was my sister-in-law from my first marriage, who flew in from Europe to be with us. We have remained very close."

of a sudden a burst of sunshine came through the clouds and poured through the huge windows into the where we were standing under the chuppah (a traditional wedding canopy). It was a very moving moment that signified to me that my first husband was there, and let me know that it was okay for me to remarry. I don't think you can avoid having guilty feelings about moving on, but make sure that they don't overwhelm you by focusing on your current happiness.

———————————

It's a good idea to talk with a relationship counselor so you can process your emotions. A few sessions may be enough to help articulate your feelings and get some clarity for the future. "With clarity comes less baggage and an honorable way to preserve the memory of the spouse you lost and begin to create a new future," says Dr. Les Parrott.

Roberta Temes, Ph.D., says widows may choose to include their first husband's family at their second wedding and even say a prayer to honor his memory. And when children are involved, she suggests taking them on a family honeymoon either before or after the wedding.

Feeling Good About Your Second Marriage

Make sure you remind yourself to think positive so you can enjoy your engagement. It probably won't be as stressful as being engaged the first time, but as with any affair, planning can be overwhelming. "People don't always get things right the first time and we have to accept that marriage may be one of those things," says Dr. Ann Rosen Spector. "It doesn't mean we are a failure or a terrible person."

It's human nature to try again. Even if you endured a bitter divorce and swore you'd never get married again, it's normal to want to make another go at marriage. According to Dr. Coche, it is a fundamental human need to be touched, acknowledged by another, and "have one's life witnessed. Partnering satisfies something inherently and fundamentally human for many people," she says.

Second-timers are privy to an enormous amount of life experience. I remember thinking that I felt very old at age 28 following my divorce. I aged emotionally and learned first-hand that relationships can come undone no matter how good your intentions are. But why

> ## Wedding Day Reflections
>
> I was 24 at my first wedding and now at 38, as I plan my California beach wedding, I'm more interested in a feel-good day with friends and family. My second wedding will be a true party. I've already been through a wedding, so I am not that concerned with things like the perfect white wedding dress, a full-size wedding party, or a veil.
>
> —Marla

mope? I've learned to make light of situations that are initially painful. It's all how you look at things. We second-time sisters have had time to reflect on our past. Maybe it took us a while to get the right guy, but now we know we just saved the best for last!

Don't get caught in the mind-set that a wedding is supposed to be once in a lifetime, so why should you be entitled to another one? Take it from me—that's a crock! Your second marriage has no relation to your first, so why shouldn't you be able to celebrate with the ceremony and party of your dreams?

What Will People Think?

Your life is interesting—people will talk. So what? Once you block out the whisper of people referencing your first breakup, you can move on with your life and do what's best for you. In a minute they'll be talking about someone else anyway. That is, of course, unless you plan to have an underwater wedding in full scuba gear. Then they'll be back talking about you! But second-time brides don't care what people think of their wedding plans the way first-time brides do. Some say first weddings are more about show and less about the couple. First-time brides are trying to please everyone, from their parents and future in-laws to their sorority sisters and second-grade teacher.

Professionally Speaking

The second-time bride needs to realize that she doesn't have to worry about what other people are thinking. A marriage and ceremony are rites of passage that involve the community.

—Ann Rosen Spector, Ph.D.
www.annrosenspectorphd.com

"I was so consumed with tradition, what society would think, and what my parents would pay for, when I got married the first time," says Cheryl Mayfield Brown, 38, owner of Twice Is Nice Encore Bridal Creations (www.twiceisnicebride.com) a wedding coordinating, consulting, and bridal-show business for encore couples based

How Can I Feel Good About Being a Bride Again?

- "Think through where the mistakes were if your first marriage failed, and then grow from the experience. If you did this before recoupling, then it is easy to love again and enjoy a second wedding." –Dr. Judith Coche

- "Know in your heart that you are making a wise choice." –Dr. Roberta Temes

- "Make a list of 'shoulds' that are causing you to feel most guilty. For example, you may feel that you should not wear a white dress, or you should not accept gifts, or you should not have a traditional ceremony. Review the list with someone objective (a counselor can help) and they will help you see that your list of 'shoulds' is probably unjustified and unproductive." –Dr. Les Parrott

- "Concentrate on how lucky and blessed you are to have found love." –Dr. Judith Coche

- "Accept the support of family and friends. If people care about you, then they want to be there for the good times." –Dr. Ann Rosen Spector

in Charlotte, North Carolina. "Being experienced and more mature, I didn't care what people thought when I planned my second wedding."

Chances are you've incorporated some alternative ideas into your affair and you're proud. Your attitude is, "Let them talk—this time I'm getting married my way." You don't have the energy to waste on such pettiness as people gossiping about this being your "second marriage." You've been through severe emotional pain—whether a divorce or a death—and you know what's important now. It's not about the ring, the dress, or the number of bridesmaids by your side. It's about the love, respect, devotion, and commitment between you and your groom. You found love again and you have every right to dance the night away.

And while you're shaking your groove thing and not caring about what people think, be thankful that we live in a more forgiving time. Decades ago, women remarried only if their husbands died, and it was still a quiet gathering where she didn't wear a wedding gown or virginal white. But with the high divorce statistics today, second weddings are fairly common.

Even five years ago, people were more uptight about the do's and don'ts, according to Eileen Livers, vice president of editorial programming at iVillage.com, who oversees all content for the Web site, including wedding articles and message boards. "I think there is a little bit more of an understanding for second marriages and therefore a little less embarrassment, shame, or guilt about having a second wedding. Look at your wedding as a celebration of the relationship instead of focusing on what 'number' wedding it is," she says.

Wedding Day Reflections

People lose sight of what the wedding is about and are more concerned with finding out which band, florist, and photographer you're using.

—Dana

Spreading the Word (Yes, You Can Announce Your Wedding in the Newspaper)

You're probably already thinking that you can skip the impersonal formalities of sending out printed announcements along with fancy save-the-date cards. If you have a short engagement, you may feel that you'd be sending invitations just as soon as the engagement announcements hit your guests' mailboxes. Or you may think sending announcements is an unnecessary step or simply out of your budget.

But skipping such first-time bride formalities doesn't mean you can't tell the world that you're getting married. You just need to enlighten certain people before word gets out on the street that you're getting hitched. The first people to tell are your children. They cannot hear from Grandma or your next-door-neighbor that you are getting married. It's important that you do this in private rather than springing it on them in the middle of a crowded restaurant. They need time to react and be true to themselves. If they are initially upset, encourage them to express their feelings and reassure them that you love them and are always there for them.

You'll probably want to tell your parents right away, but if you have children, don't let them announce the news to their friends until you've broken the news to your ex-husband. You need to tell him before he hears it from the kids. If you don't have kids, and you are friendly with your ex, go ahead and give him the news. If you are not in touch with your ex, then it's not necessary to pick up the phone out of the blue just to say, "Hi, I hope you've been well the last seven years—I'm getting married."

You'll probably want to inform the rest of your family and your friends with a phone call. It's fun to hear your best friend in California scream with excitement on the other end of the line. These priceless moments are not just reserved for the first-time bride. Your family and friends are going to want the scoop on how your fiancé proposed and then they'll ask the inevitable, "Have you set a date?"

Second-time brides often have fewer guests at their wedding, and I repeatedly hear that it's because they want to be surrounded by only their closest friends and family. As for work colleagues and other peripheral people, you can send an e-mail sharing your news.

You absolutely can announce your engagement and/or wedding in the local newspaper. Be sure you have a great recent photo. Just call the newspaper and ask what information they require in order to print your announcement. They are not going to ask how many times you've been married! It will be fun to save the clipping for your wedding scrapbook to look back on with your children and grandchildren.

The excitement about being a second-time bride has kicked in. It's time to start planning your magical day!

Coordinating Your Concept

Picturing the Time, Place, and Style of Your Wedding

Many brides say that when they think about their first wedding, they remember the chaos surrounding all of the planning. Now, for the second wedding, the bride wants to remember the meaning, and wants the planning to reflect who she and the groom are as individuals and as a couple. You can create a magical wedding that is as big or small, formal or funky as you like because there are no rules. Second weddings often include personalized ingredients, whether it's poetic vows, a special love song you wrote for the occasion, or a creative invitation that represents your shared hobbies.

In the Beginning

Perhaps, way back at wedding number one, your mom or another relative put all of your plans into motion. Maybe she even came up with the plans. She wanted the band her friends used and the florist her neighbor raved about. But this time, it's your turn to take the lead—working the phones and surfing the Internet to line up the vendors of your choice. But before you get down to hiring them (more about that in chapter 6), you need to think about what you are trying to achieve.

Depending on the magazine or expert, you might get different advice about which planning steps need to get done first. Some say you need your guest list before you can plan a thing, while others say it's important to first figure out the type of wedding you want. Well, both are true. You have to do what works best for you. Such freedom is hardly addressed in first weddings. The huge bridal magazines all run pages-long checklists of things you need to do starting 12 months before the wedding and up to the very minute you exchange vows. Not meeting a certain item on the agenda could bring a beginner bride to tears!

Fortunately, there are no rigid rules when it comes to a second wedding. Go ahead and do things out of order—it will probably feel good. But if you need help getting started, here are some tips:

• *Do Your Research.* Regardless of how many times you get married, the first steps in planning are always the same: Figure out the type of wedding you want and the time of year you want to get married, and then start calling places to research prices and availability. Ask around and find out who other brides are using. Look beyond the number of associations vendors belong to or how much press they've received, and get recommendations from people. You'll learn more about the entire experience of working with the vendor from beginning to end. Part of your research is comparing packages, prices, and personalities of vendors, and most of all, talent. My husband and I were so impressed by our photographer's work that we overlooked the fact that he was not warm and fuzzy and we went with him anyway.

• *Get Organized.* Buy a three-ring binder and make it your new best friend. It's true that there are many ready-made planners on the bookstore shelves—large, heavy hardcover books with files perfectly categorized for the bride-to-be. So why buy a binder? Before you get ready to lug such "organizers" home, realize these files are geared toward first-time brides. You need to create your own categories, such as clothing, flowers, music, and photography. You may also want a section for extras, and file pockets to hold brochures and clippings from magazines. It's also good to have a budget section to keep track of your spending and to have lined paper to record different quotes you receive from various vendors, along with the name of the person you spoke with and the date of your conversation.

Should You Hire a Wedding Coordinator?

I've heard many stories of brides who didn't know where to turn when they started planning their second wedding. Comments from recent second-time brides include: "I found wedding information designed for the first-time bride" and "I couldn't find articles that spoke to the younger second-time bride. Everything I read catered to women with children or women who wouldn't have a big wedding."

If you find there isn't enough information, consider hiring a wedding coordinator who has experience with second weddings. At the least, he or she may be able to tell

Professionally Speaking

According to the Association of Bridal Consultants, brides older than age 30 are more likely to use a wedding consultant than are younger brides.

you how other brides have handled situations such as wording the invitations or deciding what to wear. And if you want someone else to work the phones and narrow down your options, from which valet service to hire to which hairstylists will come to your hotel room the day of your wedding, a wedding coordinator may be a good call for you.

Though you may feel you don't need a wedding coordinator because you've done it all before, keep in mind that a wedding coordinator can be your mediator, negotiator, therapist, and stylist all in one. A recent bride explains that her wedding coordinator helped save her money because the coordinator gets discounts with certain vendors for doing repeat business. She also kept the bride from getting stressed out by personally dealing with each vendor. I was recently in a bridal salon with a friend while she stood in the large three-way mirror in horror because the dress was not altered to her liking. Well, she didn't have to say a word. Her wedding coordinator—who accompanies her to every vendor appointment—demanded to speak to the manager and made sure that gown was fixed.

As a second-time bride, you have been to at least a few weddings over the years and you may know exactly what you *don't* want. You may have a clear idea of what kind of décor you're after and you may also know how to execute your plans. "I have in my head already what I want and I am going to put my wedding together myself," says Marla. Another bride I interviewed said the planning is part of the fun of being engaged. She felt that she missed out by not planning her first wedding, so she is trying to enjoy every moment.

Even if you consider yourself the ultimate entertainer and you wouldn't dream of handing off the planning duties to anyone else, you might want to consider hiring a coordinator to show up at the end. She can help with the flow of the wedding so you don't have to worry about the logistics. She can make sure that your ring-bearers have their pillows and the harpist knows where to sit. "You want to be the bride and not have to worry about whether or not the food is being served, the flowers are pinned on, or the photographer is where he needs to be," says Gerard J. Monaghan, president of the Association of Bridal Consultants. "You want to bask in the joy of the day."

The Association of Bridal Consultants cites as many as 43 different types of businesses that deal with weddings, from caterers and photographers to people who offer hot-air balloon rides and dove releases. The coordinator can help you sift through the enormous number of vendors.

Wedding coordinators can also help you save money, according to Monaghan. "They know the appropriate price for menu items and flowers. They can keep you from buying things you don't need, and in some cases they can get you add-ons and discounts. The vendors work with consultants on a continual basis; it is in their best interest to offer some incentive to the consultant."

"A good consultant will do whatever the bride contracts her for, from planning the whole wedding to running the ceremony," Monaghan says. "We recommend against packages because they don't make the bride feel special. The idea is to let the bride design her own wedding so she and the coordinator can agree on a price together. Most coordinators work for a flat fee or an hourly basis. It usually comes out somewhere between 10 percent and 15 percent of the total cost of the wedding." He also adds, "Be sure to ask for references from the last three brides they worked for . . . If you ask only for *any* references, they will give you their best three."

The contract needs to specify costs, when payments are due, and who is doing what (and with whom). "The contract essentially prevents the 'Whoops, I thought you were doing that' syndrome," says Monaghan.

So do you really need a wedding coordinator? It depends who you ask. You can probably manage making the plans, but would you relax and enjoy your engagement more if somebody else followed up on the little details? And remember, a certified wedding coordinator isn't your only option. For example, some florists are now expanding their services and are designing receptions and offering ideas similar to a wedding coordinator's role. You don't necessarily need someone certified by an association. Some of the most creative and gorgeous weddings I've seen were designed or orchestrated by self-taught gurus. One florist I interviewed, whose work is featured in national magazines, never received any formal floral arrangement training and doesn't belong to any florists' professional organizations.

A Little Assistance Please!

You may want a wedding coordinator if:

- Your mom planned your first wedding and you don't know where to begin.
- You work crazy hours and have no time for the full-time job wedding planning can become.
- You are busy raising kids.
- You work, raise kids, and attend night school.
- You are out of touch with the vast wedding market (for instance, if taffeta ruffled dresses and banana hair clips were the rage for bridesmaids when you got married).

I had a wedding coordinator lead the rehearsal the day before my wedding. When you have a bunch of out-of-town friends in one room who haven't seen each other in years, someone's got to be the bad guy and raise a voice so the rehearsal happens. The coordinator also made the wedding day run smoothly. She made sure the wedding party was lined up appropriately and that everyone was where they were supposed to be for pictures. She allowed me to be the relaxed bride. At one point she even brought me a mixed drink, right on cue. Anything I wanted, she made happen.

It was important to me that my groom be the first person to see me when I went downstairs to the hotel ballroom. I was running a little late getting the finishing touches of my hair and makeup done and our bridesmaids and groomsmen were all hanging out in my direct path to where my husband-to-be was supposed to meet me. Before I knew it, the wedding coordinator excused herself and went ahead and informed the group that they couldn't see me yet. I managed to walk down the hall without anyone getting so much as a peek of my gown. I remember their voices. "Can we come out yet?" I have no idea what she did with them—they could have all been piled in a broom closet for all I know—but what mattered to me at that moment was that my groom was the first person to lay eyes on his bride.

What's Your Vision? Picking the Type of Wedding and Time of Year

Imagine the kind of wedding that would truly make you and your fiancé happy. Take that vision and build your ideas from there. Are you seeing nature-trail nuptials, a ceremony by the sea, or a party at the Plaza?

Bigger and Better (Going All Out)

If you had a small first wedding, you may be yearning for a megaparty. Or, perhaps your fiancé was never married and he wants a grand wedding. Or, maybe you both are financially prepared to throw yourselves a beautiful wedding and you don't want to leave anyone or anything out. You want to go all out!

LESLIE AND ANTHONY'S STORY

I had a big wedding the first time at age 26, but my husband did not; he just had a civil service at age 21. When it came time to plan our wedding, every magazine or etiquette book I read said I shouldn't have a big wedding, or wear white, a veil, or a train. It was frustrating. I was in my early thirties and this was the first time I was marrying this particular person. Why did I have to tone it down or be less elaborate? The wedding was to celebrate our union together and it shouldn't be less of a hoopla because it was a second wedding. We were able to add things that I didn't have at my first wedding because we were paying for the wedding ourselves and we had a bigger budget. I told him we were going all out! We had a formal sit-down dinner with a videographer, limousines, and favors— chocolate bars with tidbits about us on the wrapper.

Small and Secluded (At Home, Country Inn, Bed & Breakfast)

Many second weddings are smaller and more intimate than first weddings. The perfect place for a small wedding is a sweet country inn you visited with your fiancé on your romantic drive across the country, or in the comfort and beauty of your home, or the home you grew up in. Small and secluded weddings can be extremely elegant. You can have a formal black-tie dinner party for 12 people around your own dining room table. A formal wedding doesn't have to be a big wedding. Remember, this is the book that lets you break all the rules! Of course, at home you will have more freedom with decorating and probably with menu options, too, because you won't be required to use a certain caterer.

City Living (Bistros, Hotels, Jazz Clubs, Piano Bars, Mansions, Museums)

Whether you are the hip downtown woman or the suburban chick who *wants* the hip downtown wedding, a city-style affair may be just what you need. The prices are generally more expensive than in smaller towns, but at least it's more fun for your out-of-town guests when they need something to do during the rest of your wedding weekend. Even if your location of choice doesn't have a view of a skyline, you'll be happy as long as it is far from generic banquet halls with low ceilings and stained carpeting. Perhaps you want to explore renting out a loft, or maybe an art gallery or science museum. There are many unique venues now interested in getting a piece of the wedding market. Does the aquarium or zoo have an exhibit area or pretty lobby you can rent out? Or how about a glamorous evening at the opera house? Even little bistros or jazz clubs can create the perfect atmosphere for your nuptials. A place may not advertise that they are available for weddings, but that doesn't mean they are off limits. Make some calls and ask vendors to suggest some really distinctive city locations that other brides have used.

Wedding Day Reflections

I was only 18 at my first wedding. I planned it for a year and a half and spent tens of thousands of dollars on a reception for 350 people that I couldn't enjoy because I was so stressed out making sure everything went perfectly. For my second wedding at age 34, my goal was simplicity. We had an intimate ceremony in our living room encircled by 15 of our closest friends and family. We even included our dog in the festivities, which would have been difficult if the wedding was any place other than at home.

–Erika

Scenic (Parks, Beaches, Gardens, Mountains)

Many brides are picking the scenic route when it comes to second weddings. What could be more beautiful than pictures of you and your honey in front of a fiery sunset by the lake where you first met?

If you want an outdoor wedding during a Midwest autumn, you can bet your pictures will be so gorgeous you won't even need makeup—the candy-corn-colored foliage will be the real star. The pictures are probably one of the greatest benefits of an outdoor wedding. There is nothing like a soft, natural setting instead of a cheesy, stiff backdrop.

Maybe you are a nature lover or you and your fiancé are big hikers, and the outdoors just speaks to you. Perhaps you think having a backyard party will be more affordable than renting out a restaurant. Whatever your reasons, outdoor affairs have the potential for elegance and perfection. However, there are just a few things I'd like to point out: *Bugs. Heat. Rain.*

Allow me to elaborate. Although your pictures won't pick up the pesky mosquitos nipping at everyone at your twilight ceremony, your guests may walk away from your wedding remembering those darn bugs! And as for rain—wow, nothing can frizz your hair and freak out your mother faster than a torrential downpour on your wedding day. I'm not trying to rain on your parade myself; I just want you to be realistic when you picture your perfect day. Will it be just as magical if you have to move the entire wedding from the top of the ski slopes into the lodge because of a major snowstorm?

I was at a wedding in a small beach town where the bride and groom were planning to recite their vows barefoot in the sand by the water's edge as the sun set. But instead, the sky was a blackish gray, ready to unload on the ceremony site. Her dream of being a beach

Wedding Day Reflections

I got married right after Christmas. It was a second wedding for both of us. I just turned 40, and he is 42. We both have two children, who were present at the wedding. I have a large immediate family, so we decided to have the wedding at a restaurant with just immediate family present. A retired minister from the church I attended growing up performed the ceremony, and then we had a buffet-style dinner afterward. I didn't really want a traditional wedding—I already did that once.

—Carla

bride was not shattered, just altered. At the last minute, the location was changed to inside the tent, and then it started to pour. Guests were escorted in twos by the groomsmen holding umbrellas. When the ceremony began, you could hear the thunder and see the tent poles shaking from the storm. It was an adventure, but the bride and groom rolled with it. They didn't let anything spoil their day.

The beauty about being a second-timer is that you are so happy to be marrying your true love that you're not going to obsess over things out of your control that could easily send a first-time bride into shock.

While we're talking about the elements, I must also mention a wedding I attended in the Southern summer heat. I was in a sleeveless dress and still was ready to crawl down the aisle in search of water. My husband was dripping wet in his suit and tie. How could we pay attention to what I'm sure were beautiful vows when we were about to pass out? If you want an outdoor wedding, make sure you consider your guests and the time of year. If you are going to have a lot of kids or your 10 great-aunts, then maybe getting married outside in the middle of August shouldn't be your first choice.

Even if you have the scenic thing down to a science, consider other issues besides the weather. Do you have to rent everything from tents to toilets? Do you need to get insurance? How will people get to the top of that deserted mountain? What about the noise factor? I was at a waterfront wedding where the weather couldn't have been more perfect. The bride couldn't have been more gorgeous and the flowers couldn't have been lovelier. Then all of a sudden a motorboat roared by . . . and then another . . . and then another.

Traditional (Church, Temple, Synagogue)

Maybe you eloped the first time and now you want the church or synagogue wedding you dreamed of as a little girl. You may want a traditional ceremony even if you went that route the first time. If it's important to your fiancé to get married in a church, temple, or synagogue, you can let him have his wish without feeling like you are experiencing déjà vu. First of all, it will never be the same. Even if you repeated every planning detail from your first wedding, there is one major difference: You are marrying a different man. You can get married in a similar type of location; just do it differently. For example, if you had an outrageously big church wedding once, maybe for your second wedding, you'll repeat the church setting but tone it down.

BECKY AND JIM'S STORY

At age 26, Becky got married in a huge church with 500 people in attendance. She wore her mother's wedding dress, and her 10 brides-maids sported matching gowns, shoes, and necklaces, and carried identical flowers. For her second wedding, it was important for Jim to have a traditional ceremony surrounded by his family and friends. They decided to have their wedding in a small chapel with just family and close friends—fewer than 50 people—and then invited 200 guests to the reception afterward. The church was decorated elegantly with two small candelabras arranged with beautiful flowers. Becky had just one request: that the organist play the wedding march as she walked down the aisle with her dad.

Vegas or Bust (Eloping, Destinations)

When I think of eloping, I think of Vegas. To me, they both represent a sense of urgency and spontaneity. If you want the flip side of your first wedding in the cathedral, then maybe a jaunt to the city of sin is a fun way to tie the knot. I've heard many second-time brides say they initially considered eloping when they first got engaged. For some, it's because they just want to get married and are not concerned with having a full-fledged wedding, or even with having family and friends witness their union, for that matter. Sometimes it's just easier to make a getaway. The months of pre-wedding worries from how to word the invitations to who should walk down the aisle with Grandma are nonexistent.

But if you want a little of both—the closeness of family and friends, but the excitement of a distant location—you need to make some calls or surf the Internet to see about how and where to set up your wedding from afar. If you are up for something a little more exotic, you may find yourself doing more planning than you bargained for. Destination weddings involve booking airfare, hotels, and transportation, in addition to hiring people to handle the food and décor as well as the ceremony. You also need to realize that you may not meet any of these people, who will be responsible for the major elements of one of the most important days of your life, until your wedding day.

Hiring a wedding coordinator for her destination wedding was a necessity for Missy, who found her coordinator through the Web site www.weddingsinthebahamas.com. "Our planner is picking us up at our hotel and taking us to the government of-

Wedding Day Reflections

Both my husband and I had been married before and we wanted to do something really special for our wedding. We decided to get married abroad. Neither of us had ever been to Paris before—we both traveled extensively, but were each saving Paris for "that special someone." When we realized that each of us was the other's "special someone," we knew Paris was the place for us. His daughter joined us and I arranged the whole thing via the Internet.

—Sharon

fice to assist us in obtaining our marriage license," says Missy. "She made the arrangements with the hotel, minister, florist, and photographer. All we have to do is show up! It's great—like having your mom help you without the pressure to do what she wants you to do."

Choosing the Date

While you are thinking about where you'd like to get married and whom you'd like around you, also think about when to set the date. Have a couple of backup dates in case your first choice isn't available. And remember, it's always wise to avoid getting married during the same month you married your ex.

SENTIMENTAL DATES

Do you want to get married on the anniversary of your first date or on the same day your parents tied the knot? Do you have a favorite holiday you've always thought would be perfect for a wedding?

SEASON YOU LIKE

Did you sweat through your first wedding in the August heat? Do you want pictures with fall foliage in the background and no humidity? Do some seasons mesh better with your work schedule than others? Teachers like to get married in the spring, while my brother, who is a certified public accountant, had no desire to get married in March or April. But tax season aside, he needed a holiday weekend for the convenience of his out-of-town guests, so he chose Memorial Day weekend.

School and Kids' Schedules

If you plan to get married during your son's Little League playoffs, watch out. Or, if your kids are taking finals in December or the spring, don't get married around that time. The same applies if they attend overnight camp in the summer. And don't be sneaky and plan the wedding during the kids' vacation time with their dad so he gets jipped on his weekend.

Officiant's Availability

Consider certain religious holidays, times of the year, days of the week, and even times of the day that your officiant won't perform the ceremony. For example, if you want a Saturday night wedding and your rabbi celebrates the Sabbath, then he will not be able to drive to your ceremony site until sundown. In the summer that means starting the wedding quite late.

You've pictured your dream wedding. You've explored the many different types of places possible, from city mansions to scenic mountains. Whether morning or evening, indoors or outdoors, winter or spring, you have exciting options and it's time to start planning. Remember the reason you're making such special plans. This isn't going to be any ordinary day—it's your wedding!

Oh Joy!

THE MONEY TALK

You've envisioned your ideal wedding—it's grand—and it's going to cost gazillions. Now back to reality. Can you believe how expensive weddings have become just since your first wedding? You want to make sure your second wedding is beautiful and special, but how do you get what you want without giving up too much?

You don't have to let go of your vision; you just have to tweak it. Finding the money may be as easy as shuffling a few things around. You've done your research and know how much the photographer costs and how much you must come up with to re-create the floral designs you've seen in *In Style* magazine. You can achieve your dream wedding by prioritizing what's most important to you. If you absolutely want a Saturday night affair, you may have to invite fewer guests. If atmosphere is most important to you, rent the restaurant/museum/opera house of your dreams at an off-peak time. Decide to do without the charger dinner plates, French envelopes, Chiavari chairs (ballroom chairs that are considered the nicest and priciest), and super-sized wedding cake.

Years ago, it was understood that for a first wedding, the bride's family paid for pretty much everything except the marriage license, rehearsal dinner, and perhaps corsages for the mothers. The groom, of course, was expected to take care of his bride financially, forever. So all the other costs, including the reception site, liquor, food, cake, band, gratuities, invitations, photographer, videographer, flowers, and transportation—for starters—were left for the lucky father of the bride.

Bridal publications estimate that 50 percent of the budget is usually spent on the reception, leaving 10 percent each for music, flowers, and photography. The remaining 20 percent is for attire (dress, headpiece, lingerie, jewelry, shoes, hair and makeup, groom's clothes), invitations, programs, rings, officiant's fee, attendants' gifts, wedding gifts for each other, marriage license, rehearsal dinner, and more, depending on how many extras you want to include.

Of course these figures are directed toward first-time brides, and most weddings run 10 percent over budget. Adjust your numbers accordingly. You should also keep in mind that many magazines and Internet sites report averages. Chances are the picture of the gorgeous gown you tore out of the magazine does not cost $800 (the average spent on a dress), but instead is a designer dress that costs $2,000.

Second-Time Smarts

If you want some second-time savings, skip the items that are often considered silly little extras. You don't need to buy a throw-away bouquet or garter, favors, bridesmaids' gifts, or bags of send-off fragrant dried flowers, let alone a silk Shantung guest book. Don't spend money on little silver-plated clocks that your friends would never dream of displaying in their homes. For the more sophisticated second wedding, the emphasis is on the core elements of the wedding: the ceremony, the ambiance, the music.

A Wedding's Little Surprises

Once you determine your budget, decide where to spend the bulk of your money. A great thing about second weddings is that you are not tied to doing the expected. You don't have to go the traditional route and buy 30 floral centerpieces and order 300 chicken dinners. You can throw in some surprises and adjust your budget accordingly.

BETH AND SCOTT'S STORY

We planned and paid for our own wedding at a private dining club in a five-star hotel on a Saturday night in Chicago. My first wedding was larger but it was less expensive. The wedding was in Wisconsin, where everything is more reasonable, and it was at a synagogue on a Sunday night, which also lowered the cost. But even with a bigger budget, my first wedding wasn't nearly as elegant as my second wedding, which was smaller and more intimate. Since Scott and I paid for our wedding ourselves, it gave us the freedom to make our own decisions (the synagogue setting at my first wedding was to please my mom). Also, the fact we were in our thirties (I was 26 at my first wedding) gave us the ability to have the kind of wedding we wanted. We could be more creative and spend more in areas that were important to us. We wanted something different. We did not spend a fortune on flowers. The room had windows overlooking the city skyline and it already had quite a bit of color. We

> ## Second-Time Smarts
>
> Second-time brides usually have fewer attendants. Instead of buying so-so flowers for 12 bridesmaids, you can spend more money on exotic flowers for your three sisters.

liked the simple décor and decided to place our emphasis on the food. We probably spent 80 percent of our budget on food, wine, and alcohol. We spent a lot of time picking out fabulous food. The chef from our favorite sushi restaurant in Chicago prepared and presented the sushi. We even gave the hotel chef a recipe for a dish we loved from a restaurant in Los Angeles. We had lots of food stations set up but we didn't have assigned seating. We designed it like an elegant cocktail party with cabaret-style tables spread out, but we purposely didn't have enough tables for everyone. People seemed to really like the fact that it was so social. Everyone mixed and mingled more than if they were committed to sitting with one group of people for the whole evening. We both had experienced many weddings where you're seated at a "boring" table and you are stuck making small talk all night. Our friends still talk about how good the food was! It was worth the expense.

How to Set Your Budget and Determine Who Will Pay

Who pays for what can vary from couple to couple, depending on their combined income and also the financial situation of both families. The important thing to remember is that there are no set rules. If you and your fiancé aren't financially secure, one or both sets of parents may want to pay for the wedding. If you are older and further along in your career, you may be able to pay for your wedding or contribute. My husband and I contributed to several areas, especially the things we cared most about. Our priority was the photos. We wanted a specific photographer, so we paid part of his costs and my parents paid the other portion. The cake was lower on our list. We weren't having a formal cake-cutting ceremony and we felt that spending a fortune on a cake that no one really looks at was ridiculous. We just chose a cake offered by the hotel caterer.

Because weddings are so expensive, many families split costs today, but there are always those parents of the groom who just won't budge from paying only for the rehearsal dinner. Some parents of the groom don't wait to be asked to help out. They call the bride's parents and set up a dinner date to discuss wedding finances. It's awkward, but it needs to be done.

Figuring out what you have to spend and whose money you're spending are tough and crucial decisions that must be made early in the wedding planning process. You can research until you have stacks of caterers' catalogs and hotel brochures towering higher than a six-tier cake, but if you can't pay for it, you don't get it. Good-bye gardenias and engraved invitations.

Though outlining a wedding budget is hard, sticking to it is harder. When caterers and bridal salon salespeople are trying to sell you the best of everything, you may feel you can afford only the mediocre. But you still can't help but *want* the $10,000 dress and the shrimp and caviar hors d'oeurves.

Before you start banging your head against the table, put down your calculator and ask yourself these questions:

- How much do you have to spend?
- How much do you want to spend?
- What aspects of the wedding are most important to you and your partner?
- Do you want to have gourmet food and stark décor?
- Would you rather spend the majority of your budget on the entertainment?
- Does the cake have to be covered in hand-made sugar flowers?

Your priorities help determine the level of service you want. You may yearn for thousands of dollars' worth of flowers, but if you'd rather spend the bulk of your budget on a fabulous cake, you'll use a generic floral chain instead of a prestigious top floral designer.

Let's Keep the Love Alive

Don't let money come between you and your groom. You get angry that he doesn't want to pay for extra rose petals to throw on the ground because you feel you must walk through a sea of rose petals as you make your entrance at the ceremony. You feel that you don't want him to skimp on what is supposed to be a sacred day for you both. He doesn't want you to waste money that could help with major life expenses in the future. Money is one of the main reasons for conflict in marriages, so start opening the lines of communication now.

And don't:

• Go into debt because you thought it would be great to hire the $10,000 band that is all the rage now.

• Try to compete with anyone else. It's not important who you hire or how many people you have, so long as you are happy celebrating your marriage with those you love.

• Be in such a rush to hire people that you don't read the fine print. Make sure you understand the contract completely before you sign.

• Let your budget be the source of fights between you and your fiancé. You need to learn how to talk about money without it leading to a battle every time.

• Assume that because Mom and Dad paid for your first wedding, they don't want to contribute to this one. They may be thrilled for you, adore your fiancé, and want to help you both attain your special day. Swallowing a little pride and accepting some assistance can lift a huge financial burden from you both.

Footing the Bill

One difference between first-time brides and second-time brides is that a greater number of second-time brides and their grooms pay for the wedding themselves. Many second-time couples are older and more established in their careers, and they have the means to pay for a wedding. Some just feel that their parents have done enough and they want to pay for this wedding themselves. In other cases, it's simply about control. If the folks offer to foot the bill, then they are entitled to have a say when it comes to making decisions. It's rare for parents to hand over a blank check and say, "Do whatever you want." Those who do may find their money is spent on a wedding in Tahiti that they can't even attend because Dad doesn't fly. For brides who already went through one wedding with Mom, it might be better for your sanity to say, "Thanks, but no thanks" and just have a smaller wedding based on what you can afford.

The Money Talk

If you don't think you can afford a wedding and your parents or future in-laws don't offer to help, you may need to ask them for assistance. Each of you should privately approach your family to discuss the delicate subject of money. This is a sensitive topic and you want your parents to be able to speak freely. And, of course, if there is already enough tension between you and your future in-laws, you won't have trouble sitting this one out.

It's likely that Mom and Dad will need to be educated on how much weddings cost now. Maybe your wedding right out of college cost $15,000; today, a similar affair could run $50,000. Don't be surprised if your parents experience sticker shock. Receptions generally now cost $50 to $150 or more per person. The Association of Bridal Consultants says the national average for the cost of a wedding reception is $4,217, but consider that the number reflects the average throughout the country, and there are more small weddings than big weddings. In New York City, an elegant hotel reception for 100 people could cost $150 to $350 per person, plus roughly $10,000 to $20,000 for a band, $10,000 for flowers, and $5,000 for photography. The range varies, of course, depending on where you live and how much you want to spend for each vendor. In Los Angeles and San Francisco, an elegant hotel reception for 100 people could cost $30,000 for the reception site, food, liquor, and flowers alone.

How to Save Before Your Wedding

Michael Randel, C.P.A., managing partner of Dickson, Randel & Co., P.C., based in Royal Oak, Michigan, says you have to be conscious of saving for your wedding at all times, because there isn't much time to save. Be realistic about your budget and stick to it. Don't think, *What's another $300?* when the wedding is already costing $30,000. When your future spouse says the room would look even better with chair covers, or the caterer says for a little more money you can upgrade to a *better* sweets table, just say no.

Randel, who also does financial planning for young couples, advises having your money saved three months prior to the wedding. "It will allow you a huge safety net," he says. "There are a lot of add-ons at the end that you don't know are coming no matter how prepared you are."

Here's how other couples saved:

- Put all of your change into a jar and designate it as your honeymoon fund.
- Stop buying clothes during your entire engagement period and put the money you saved toward your wedding dress.

- Eat in (and that doesn't mean getting take-out).
- Skip the iced mocha and make coffee at home.
- Write a check to yourself each week and put it in a savings account for your wedding.
- Pay charge card bills right away to avoid late fees.
- Stop buying all the fashion magazines on the newsstand looking for dress, hair, and makeup ideas; instead, buy subscriptions for only two or three.

If you don't have much time to squirrel your money away before your wedding, there are ways you can hang onto the money you already have. You can have a beautiful, elegant reception without spending a fortune. Here are some ways to save:

1. Invite fewer guests—a smaller affair costs less.

2. Strategically time your wedding. If you have a brunch, tea, or cocktail reception, you will spend considerably less than if you have a sit-down dinner, and the rent may be less if you don't need the site during a mealtime.

3. Have your wedding on Friday or Sunday, which will usually get you better rates for locations and vendors. Saturdays are the most expensive and hardest to come by. Some first-time brides are engaged for two years just so they can book their Saturday night in June.

4. Know that holiday weekends will cost more. They are in demand, and hotel rooms for your guests will be pricey and scarce. Also avoid big-event weekends in the area, such as homecoming weekend in a college town.

Wedding Day Reflections

My fiancé and I banked one of our paychecks, and we lived together first. Sharing living expenses and using one salary for the bills and the other for wedding expenses was a great saving solution.

        –Leslie

5. Consider the month. Costs escalate during peak wedding months—May, June, September, and October.

6. Hire a wedding coordinator. She will often get the best prices from bands, caterers, and reception sites because she brings them repeat business. She also knows how to make sure you don't pay hidden costs.

7. Look for a beautiful dress in a boutique or department store before you visit bridal salons. A dress not designated as a "wedding gown" is likely to cost less.

8. Knock an hour off the length of your reception. If you are paying certain vendors by the hour, this will help cut costs without sacrificing elegance.

9. Don't have the band play overtime. One couple was charged $1,500 for the extra hour at the end of the wedding.

10. Skip the fancy cake by a special cake designer. Use fresh flowers for decoration instead of sugar flowers, which take a lot of work to create.

11. Select flowers that are in season or that can be purchased in the United States. Flowers that need to be shipped from overseas cost more.

12. Avoid the day for lovers. Scheduling your wedding within a week of Valentine's Day will mean higher prices for flowers. Not only are the florists swamped; flower wholesalers charge the florists more then, which means you pay more.

Mom, It's My Wedding!

Even if your mother isn't paying for this affair, she may still feel it is her role to help you make the "right" decisions. You don't have to get angry. It's nice that she is interested and wants to be involved in your wedding. I know some parents who wouldn't care if their children eloped.

HALLIE'S STORY

For my second wedding, at age 31, I planned the huge fairy tale wedding I had always dreamed of with all the bells and whistles. It wasn't the wedding my mother wanted. I was 23 at my first wedding and my mom made all of the decisions because she and my dad paid for it. When I planned my second wedding, my mother gave me grief telling me that it was inappropriate to have a big wedding because I'd been married before. Even though my fiancé and I were paying for our own wedding, she was not happy to learn that it would not be her style wedding. Signing the checks allowed me to take control!

Hallie's folks paid for her post-college first wedding "on a shoestring budget." Her second wedding was larger and more upscale all the way around:

Wedding #1

Total Budget: $5,000

What She Got: University chapel ceremony, university reception catered by university kitchen ("the worst food you can imagine"), cases of beer and jugs of wine, silk flowers, out-of-focus pictures from Dad's camera.

Wedding #2

Total Budget: $25,000

What She Got: Elegant church ceremony, harpist, pink and yellow roses, country club reception, 300 guests, open bar, great

Professionally Speaking

It is important to make the families feel involved. Consider their thoughts and opinions but make your own decisions. Perhaps your mother can help you with the guest list or shop with you for your dress, and maybe your future mother-in-law can plan the rehearsal dinner.

—Carol Marino, president and owner of A Perfect Wedding, an event planning business in Washington D.C.

food, ice sculptures, photographer, videographer, limousines, valet parking, babysitter on premises.

While we are on the subject of motherly intervention, know that you don't have to be open to your mother's taste—unless of course you like her taste. I'm actually a big fan of my mom's ability to add beauty to anything she touches. I have learned a lot about style and décor from my mom. She has a great eye, and it just so happened that when she showed me an idea of a color scheme for my second wedding, from a page she tore out of a magazine, I agreed with her right away. The jewel-tone colors were so magnificent that one of her friends marched into her florist's shop with pictures from my wedding and said she wanted the same colors for her daughter's wedding. What a nice compliment!

And now it's your turn for praise. I know you'll create the elegant wedding of your dreams without surpassing your budget. You're smart, creative, and ready to celebrate!

Making the Cut

The Guest List

The guest list can depend on your budget or the type of wedding you want. Maybe you want only 20 people at your wedding. Maybe you want 120 people but your budget allows only 75. If that's the case, you need to decide who will make the cut.

The older you get, the easier it is to make the necessary cuts. You, your parents, your ex, or his parents may have felt obligated to include certain guests at the first wedding, but you are not getting married to make sure other people are happy. This time you and your fiancé should be happy with your wedding and about the decisions leading up to the big day.

You're not 22 and fresh out of college. You are established in your career and you are secure in the person you've become. You have grown, but you've learned the hard way that not all of your friends have grown with you. Perhaps you've grown apart from some of the guests (and maybe even some of the bridesmaids) from your first wedding.

You now know who your through-thick-and-thin friends are, and they are not always the people you swore would be your best friends for life back at your prom in 1986. You may have found from experiencing the major life change of divorce or losing your husband that your friends showed their true colors. I had a friend for years who was not supportive when I got divorced. She was more concerned with the fact that I didn't tell her that my ex and I were having problems than with helping me through the pain of having my personal life completely unravel at the seams. Needless to say, I didn't feel I had to invite her to my second wedding just because we go way back.

Jane Who?

I can't tell you how many brides have joked about the number of guests they didn't even know at their first wedding. They had an al-

First Choice or Runner-Up?

Here is a practice I consider quite tacky: Creating an "A" list and then a "B" list of your guests. You send out the "A" invitations first, and when some response cards come back as "no" you send out invitations to people on the "B" list. Now, what if someone on the "B" list hears about the wedding from someone on the "A" list, who received an earlier invitation? Wouldn't this person wonder why the invitation eventually showed up three weeks later? It's best to just invite as many people as you want and can afford. If some of them can't come, you have more money to spend in other areas.

bum filled with pictures of people who were almost strangers. Those smiling faces weren't one bit special to them. When parents pay for the wedding, they usually create the list and tell you and your fiancé how many slots are open for your guests.

Often with first weddings, your parents feel they have to include everyone from the community—including coworkers, neighbors, and acquaintances from church or temple—because they don't want to hurt anyone's feelings by leaving some people out. They also make it a habit to invite distant relatives. (Someone should write a book on where to draw the line within families.) At my first wedding there were distant cousins I've hardly spoken to my whole life. But my parents made the call. I think they wanted to include everyone in the family. My family isn't huge, so it wasn't an out-of-hand situation, but I've heard hilarious stories about weddings where the entire community is invited whether or not the bride likes the people.

The Ones Who Won't Make the List

In any case, you can forget about inviting your fourth cousins and great-great aunts and uncles, unless you are close to them. But if you are having a smaller wedding this time, you will have to cut the list, and some relatives will be left out. This gets sticky when they were invited the first time. They may wonder if they did something to upset you in the past several years; why else would they have been invited to your first wedding but not to your second? Were they important to you then but not now? This is how some family members think. Dealing with family can be very complicated. It's hard to please everyone, so don't even try. If Aunt Doris can't understand why you left out cousins George and Meg, and decides to campaign to get them on the list by calling your mother, grandmother, fiancé, and future mother-in-law, you might want to consider eloping!

I've heard of some couples who avoid such headaches without assuming much risk. They send invitations knowing that many of the out-of-town relatives won't be able to come. "A lot of people couldn't make it to our wedding because we chose to have it on a Friday night," says one bride.

When You Pay, Do Your Parents Get a Say?

When you and your fiancé are paying for the wedding, both of your parents get a say if you say so. But it's unrealistic for any of the parents to expect to invite 100 guests in this case.

What About Exes?

What about exes—are they in or out? This is a big topic, and sometimes a source of debate among couples. Your groom may want to invite his ex-wife because they are good friends and he doesn't want to be rude by not including her. You may feel that your ex-husband should be there because you have such a great relationship. But it could be very awkward for your parents, who are now accepting another man as their son-in-law. It could also be strange for your friends, and he may feel uncomfortable. But most important, how would your fiancé feel? Even if he doesn't mind if you meet your ex for lunch now and then, does your ex need to be at your wedding? Wedding etiquette experts will tell you not to invite your ex, especially if you have children. It could be confusing for them. They may act distant toward your husband-to-be because they don't want to hurt their father's feelings. It all gets very complicated. The consensus among most wedding gurus is *not* to invite your former spouse. Of course, for couples who don't care for their exes, this isn't an issue.

What About Single Friends with Dates?

If a guest isn't married but is living with his or her significant other, then they should be invited together. But if your guest isn't in a serious relationship, you have to decide what your budget and conscience can live with. I've been to many weddings where the single people are all stuck at a table in the back of the room, forced to chitchat with the stranger in the tux to their right. I have friends who were offended when they were invited to a wedding that didn't include an invitation for a date. But I've also spoken to couples who don't feel they should have to pay $100 for someone they don't know or care about. Or perhaps they would love to invite their friends with dates, but then they have to do that for everyone, and that can ruin your bud-

> ## Wedding Day Reflections
>
> We paid for our wedding so the invitation list was partly based on our budget. We just started listing everyone we wanted to come and left about 30 open slots for our parents to invite friends they felt were important to include.
>
> —Christine

get. I think it's a personal choice between you and your fiancé, but you have to agree. You can't tell your friend from high school to bring a date and then get mad if he tells his buddies from work that they can bring dates.

And what about relatives with dates? If your Aunt Rita is single, do you invite her with a date so she'll be able to enjoy herself more and have someone to dance with? If you don't want one of Aunt

Rita's rambunctious biker friends at your Sunday brunch wedding at your future in-laws' country club, that's your choice. You are the one who has to deal with the ramifications and the politics.

The List

You want to narrow your list down to people you can really call friends. A good rule, even for first weddings, is no acquaintances. It's a sure way to help you whittle your list. Remember that rule when you are sitting across from your future spouse, each of you glaring at the other with your lists in hand, waiting to see who will give up a name first. The showdown could go on all night unless you have a better method for agreeing on who makes the list. My advice is simple: You don't have to invite people just because you are in touch with them. You may have some friends you see often at the gym, or some childhood friends who you see at the coffee shop, but it doesn't mean they need to be invited to your wedding. If you feel awkward not inviting them, just explain that you are having a small wedding.

Wedding Day Reflections

I had smooth sailing with my wedding planning except when it came to the guest list. When I told my family that not all of my stepsiblings were invited, there was quite a hullabaloo. Most of my stepsiblings don't know that I exist and don't even recognize my kids as family!

—Janice

People You *Don't* Have to Invite

• *College chums.* Unless they are your close friends, you don't have to send an invitation to everyone in your sorority. Sure, they were with you for the good and the bad times, they were your family away from home, but that was 10 years ago and they probably wouldn't expect to be invited anyway. If you haven't sent them a holiday card in three years or they don't even know your fiancé's name, then you can cross them off the list right now.

- *Distant relatives.* Even if your parents feel compelled to invite them, you can skip sending out invitations to your fourth cousin through marriage and other distant relatives you've met only once in your entire life.

- *Your therapist.* Yes, she knows you better than anyone (pre-fiancé, even pre–husband number one), but how awkward would that be?

- *Your future stepbrother-in-law's in-laws.*

- *Your new friend from yoga.* If you haven't shared a meal and she's never met anyone in your family let alone your fiancé, you can forget her.

- *Work colleagues.* You do not have to invite work colleagues just because you see them every day and they've heard you talk incessantly about your wedding plans for the past four months. Besides, if they are just work friends, it probably would be uncomfortable for them to be invited to an event where you're the only person they know.

- *Kids.* With the exception of your children, future stepchildren, nieces, and nephews, you don't have to include little ones.

Wedding Day Reflections

My second wedding was fairly small in comparison to my first wedding right out of college, which was more of a bash. This time we invited only really close friends and relatives. We had about 120 people. It was my husband's first wedding, so he had a few more friends there than I did. I felt comfortable inviting only really close friends, but I felt that he deserved to have everything he wanted, which meant not limiting his guests. My in-laws did not mind not being able to invite many people to the wedding because they had a separate party for us a few months before and got to celebrate with all of their friends. I don't think my mom felt bad not inviting her friends because many of them had been to our first wedding. Also, my dad had passed away since that time, and many of my mom's friends are newer friends who understood that we were having a small wedding.
—Beth

Even though you see your friends' and cousins' kids often at barbeques and birthday parties, this is a different type of event. If you are having an indoor, formal affair, that might be tough for little kids to tolerate anyway. And if your list is already too long, stick to a no-kids policy and have a few babysitters' names handy.

• *Boss.* Do you really want to be stressed out at your own wedding? Enough said.

• *People whose weddings you've attended.* Now this gets people every time. There is an innate need to reciprocate when we are invited somewhere. Well, take into consideration that the weddings you were invited to may have been larger, first weddings. If your wedding or your budget is small, don't feel you must invite every couple who ever invited you to their wedding. Chances are you haven't kept in touch with all of them anyway. Even if your budget is unlimited, don't put them on the list just because you gave them a gift and now it's your turn. Think about who you really want to see in your pictures 20 years from now.

• *People whose wedding parties you've been in.* You may think there is an unspoken code that says you have to reciprocate, but there isn't, and you don't.

• *Neighbors.* Are you neighborly and just making conversation, or do you get together socially? If you've been in their home only to borrow sugar, they probably wouldn't be considered close friends.

• *Your parents' friends.* If you don't know who your parents' friends are or don't really care who they are, then forget extending an invitation to them. If, however, you've called your mom's best friend Auntie Ann your whole life, you probably want her at your wedding. I really wanted my parents' close friends at my second wedding. Even though they were at my first wedding, they were there for my parents when I got divorced, and I know they were truly happy for me when I found love again and announced my engagement. I've also known my parents' close friends my whole life and I can't imagine them not being at any of our important family celebrations.

Three Receptions for One Marriage

If you are having a small destination wedding or are eloping, there will be people you care about (and maybe some you don't) who are not going to witness your marriage. You probably aren't even going to invite them. Usually there are no hard feelings when you are having a small island wedding a continent away. People who aren't immediate family understand why they don't receive an invitation, and they are usually relieved that they don't have to pay for airfare and a hotel stay in addition to your gift.

Then how can you celebrate with your friends and family? You can have a few receptions. It might sound strange at first, but it's a great way to celebrate with family and friends who are from different states. One couple opted for a destination wedding. When they returned they had two celebrations—one in the South, where the bride is from, and the other in the Midwest, where the groom lives. This way, no one had to choose whose hometown got to host the couple. Some couples decide to celebrate in large cities where the majority of their friends reside.

CAROLYN AND JONATHAN'S STORY

Deciding on our guest list was so hard. We went over our lists so many times to try to keep our wedding small. We had a lot of discussion and arguments. We were trying to make sure we didn't go overboard. We had to tell good friends and family that we just couldn't invite them, and they all understood that we were having only close friends and family. Then, we decided to have a post-nuptials party that night after the sit-down dinner, and we invited our friends and employees. We took over the whole restaurant and had the band stay late, and we kept the bar open until midnight. We made special invitations for the party, and our friends showed up ready to dance and drink. The sit-down dinner started at 5:30 and by 8:30 we were done and moved everyone upstairs to join our friends for dancing. It was perfect!

Benefits of Being a Second-Time Bride

Sure, cutting the list is a drag, but let's not forget that there are benefits of being a second-timer today:

• You don't have to head over to city hall and have a hush-hush ceremony so as not to draw attention to the fact that this isn't your first wedding, like brides of previous decades did.

• You don't have to risk losing friends by forcing them to wear matching dresses with bows, taffeta, or crinoline.

• You are high-tech. Not only can you save time by doing wedding planning research on the Internet, from checking out designer gowns to locating unique reception locations, but you can communicate with your vendors via e-mail. You may not have had an Internet connection at the time of your first wedding. Heck, the Internet may not even have been around. You played a lot of phone tag trying to call vendors from work on your lunch hour or sneaking calls every time your boss left for meetings. Just think of all the vendors you won't have to meet with in person. You can e-mail some of your questions about their services and weed out the ones who don't fit your vision or budget. I often communicated with my second wedding photographer through e-mail. It was easy and quick, and it's great to have a paper trail. You don't run into problems later when you have everything in writing. The photographer can't say he didn't get the list of people on your "must-photograph" list.

• You don't have to follow the lead of others who have gone before you, as many first-time 23-year-old brides do. They often have been to only a handful of weddings (if that) and they just end up hiring the same people other brides hire. They aren't willing to explore or do research, probably because they are simply overwhelmed by the magnitude of planning a wedding, registering, and shopping for outfits for showers and engagement parties, as well as gifts for all of the hostesses. When you are older, you have an idea of the vendors you like, so you have a short list to work with instead of walking into a bridal show cold and coming out with a mound of brochures from every hall and caterer in the tri-state area.

• You don't have to run from bar to bar and slam shots with 30 of your girlfriends sporting a wedding veil and plastic penis-shaped adornments as a "last hurrah" bachelorette bash.

• You don't have to go into debt. As a second-timer, you don't feel the need to be ridiculously lavish. (And you are more likely to stick to a budget if you are spending your own money.)

• You don't have to worry about what might go wrong. If the salad is served late or the dessert table is set up in the wrong spot, oh well. Maybe your ring bearer cries his way down the aisle or the best man gets drunk and passes out before giving his toast. What are you going to do? Smile and get on with the night. The second-time bride knows that things can and do go wrong at weddings. You can plan endlessly but you can't control every second of the day. You realize that this time, you are going to let someone else stress—like the wedding coordinator—and you'll enjoy the day!

• You don't have to watch 200 rip-roaring wasted adults do the Macarena.

• You don't have to sleep at Mom and Dad's the eve of your wedding, staring at your high-school track trophies and Shawn Cassidy posters, feeling as though you've completely regressed the night before you are supposed to become someone's wife.

• You get to look gorgeous and be the best-dressed belle at the ball twice in a lifetime!

The Early Bride Gets the Band

BOOKING THE BIG FIVE

You know your budget and the number of guests. Now it's time to book the big five:

1. The place
2. The officiant
3. The music
4. The florist
5. The photographer

The order is your call, but I suggest lining up the big five as soon as you get engaged. Sometimes you don't necessarily need an exact wedding date when you start working the phones. If you know you want a fall wedding at a certain hotel, you may decide to book your wedding around its availability. If you can picture getting married by only your childhood minister or rabbi, then you need to make sure he or she is available on your date of choice before you plan the entire party.

59

Every couple has different priorities. The one common link is that second-timers want to personalize their wedding as much as possible. That means hiring the vendors you want in the order you see fit. If you have a favorite band, worth switching your wedding date for, then you need to book it soonest. The band can be in only one place at a time, and many musicians are booked well in advance. Remember that besides other brides, you are also competing with people planning other galas, from office parties to Bar Mitzvahs, so if you are trying to secure a Saturday night at a hotel or restaurant, you've got to move fast.

I've heard from many second-time brides who say they had shorter engagements than they did for their first wedding. They usually say it's because their list of what they want at their wedding is more streamlined. They often know what kind of wedding they want even before they are engaged. It doesn't take them long to put a party together. They've entertained before, and planning this party will be a breeze.

In this chapter I'll explain what you need to know before you book the big five, from questions to ask the vendors when interviewing them to what your contracts should include. I'll get into more specifics about what each vendor will do for you (such as selecting flowers and songs) in later chapters.

You'll keep stress at a minimum by booking your main vendors early. Once you have the place, officiant, music, florist, and photographer, you can relax a bit and start thinking about some of the details. It's a great feeling when you're confident in the people you've hired to help make your wedding both beautiful and meaningful.

Booking Basics

I hope your new best buddy, the three-ring binder, is nearby. Have you been taking good notes? Do you have quotes written down from different photographers? Is the atrium at the zoo available for the September date you had in mind? Did you ask your friends or other brides which vendors they used? Were they happy with their choices? It's important to get references, but take that extra step and call the couples. Ask how their pictures turned out and how professional the photographer was all evening. Ask if the hotel staff was accommodating. Were there any glitches with the flowers? You need candid information that you can't always find from people in the wedding industry—a wedding coordinator may have certain favorites she likes to deal with, or a hotel may offer only florists who regularly handle its events.

You had certain people in mind, and you've talked to some of them on the phone. It's now time to meet them in person. But don't just show up at the hotel/florist/photographer's studio expecting to meet and chat with them. You must make an appointment first. Their days revolve around appointments, and you can't just drop in and expect to be seen. With an appointment, you can be assured you will get

Second-Time Smarts

Before you sign a contract, make sure it states current prices so the vendor won't try to charge you more if the prices increase before your wedding.

their undivided attention and that they won't leave your side if some other bride walks in the door wanting to ask questions.

If you want to research vendors further, you can save some time by checking the information and sample pictures of their work on their Web sites. They may also have fact sheets that describe the services offered. It's always a good idea to check with the Better Business Bureau for any complaints filed against the vendor.

Before you book, read all contracts and ask for samples of the vendor's work. Photographers and florists will have a portfolio of pictures, and bands will have a tape or video. Never book a band without hearing it play live first, though, because tapes can be altered and they feature only the group's best work.

You also want to make sure that the person you hire will actually be the one at your wedding. You may essentially be hiring the company, which means they may be able to send any employee to your event, including a junior-manager-in-training.

Booking the Place

Are you thinking about renting the lodge at the top of a ski slope, or a grand mansion, or an art gallery? Or are you interested in booking a chapel, country club, or hotel? The tough part about booking the place is finding an available date. Choice spots can book one to two years in advance. I got engaged at the end of April, and my second wedding was at the beginning of November. I planned my entire elegant evening wedding in less than six months (I didn't want a long engagement, and as a second-time bride, I didn't feel I needed one). I was able to have it in a charming historic hotel with lovely grounds and a gorgeous lobby. The ballroom had beautiful chandeliers and high ceilings. It had much more character than the location of my first wedding, which was in a large, barren room in a synagogue. The hotel was available the weekend we wanted, but only on Sunday night. It would be difficult for out-of-town guests because they would be traveling home on Monday, a work day, but I realized that my nearest and dearest would be at my wedding no matter what day or time I held it. And because the room hadn't been booked, we received a better price than if we had a Saturday night affair. I loved the convenience of being able to walk upstairs to my room and that the ceremony and reception were held at the same location.

The hotel/country club/hall route comes with a big perk: a banquet manager. This person works with you throughout your engagement, advising you on choosing your menu and deciding

Questions to Ask Before Booking Your Reception Site

- How many people can the site *comfortably* hold?
- How many weddings are scheduled on our wedding date?
- What is included (chairs, centerpieces, tables, tablecloths, etc.)?
- Is there a dance floor? If so, what size is it?
- Does the facility have adequate power supply for a band or DJ?
- Do you have an on-site catering service?
- May we hire an outside caterer?
- Is there air conditioning?
- Is there an area for the bridal party to get ready?
- Is there valet parking?
- Do you have liability insurance?
- Do you have any restrictions regarding décor, music, or photography?
- What time can we begin setting up?
- Is there a time when everyone must be out of the site?
- Who is responsible for cleaning up the site?
- Are gratuities included?
- What are your rates?
- What kinds of extras are not included?
- On what items is there a sales tax?
- What kind of deposit is needed to confirm, and when do you need it?
- When is the final balance due?
- What are your cancellation and refund policies?

which wines to serve. Packages that include the caterer, wait staff, bartenders, and cake baker are usually available. Such sites typically charge on a per-person basis, and you may have to meet a minimum number of guests. Regardless of the location you choose, you need to find out about its rules. Are you free to decorate to your liking or would fabric on the walls be a no-no? Are you allowed to use an outside caterer? Are there sound-level restrictions with your music, or time limits on how long people can linger in the church before another wedding crew needs to start setting up? I also recommend seeing the site set up for a wedding. Either take a peek at a wedding in progress or ask to see pictures. An empty room may seem big until you look at it filled with decorations, musicians, and 100 people carrying drinks and plates. You want an idea of how the room looks all dressed up. It will help you figure out what you need to order for flowers and decorations.

Booking Your Officiant

Your ceremony is incredibly special to you and you are not going to trust it to just anyone. You are going to make sure you feel relaxed with the person joining you and your fiancé as husband and wife. You want to feel free to be yourselves and not feel that you have to say the "right" thing. When you meet with a prospective officiant you will be asked various questions about your relationship, but remember that you are also doing your own interviewing to find an officiant that's the best fit for you and your groom.

While you are meeting face-to-face, pay attention to the officiant's voice. Is it clear, or do you detect mumbling? All eyes will be on you and your gorgeous gown, but all ears will be tuned in to the person leading your ceremony. If you want someone who exudes warmth with a touch of humor, don't settle for less! I didn't. The

Questions to Ask Before Booking Your Officiant

- Is there a limited window of time that you will be able to devote to my wedding? (Some officiants will scurry out of your ceremony and head right over to another wedding to marry a different couple. You want to make sure you don't have to follow their schedule!)

- What are your requirements or restrictions (i.e., premarital counseling)?

- What are your fees?

- What is needed to confirm my date?

- Are you willing to travel to our location (whether indoors or outdoors) to perform the ceremony?

- May we write our own vows?

- Do you allow family members or close friends to have a role in the ceremony?

- Do you give a speech or sermon?

- Do you have any rules regarding music, décor, photography, or videography? (Some officiants don't want a camera flashing during the ceremony.)

ceremony was one of my favorite parts of the wedding and I credit much of it to the wonderful rabbi, who happens to be a phenomenal speaker.

If you've decided on a religious ceremony, you are probably aware that different religions have different requirements regarding remarriage. For example, if you are planning to get married in the Catholic Church, you need to allow time to get an annulment. There may also be different requirements within each religion. For example, in Judaism, Orthodox and many Conservative rabbis require a "get" (a Jewish formal divorce document signed by your ex-husband) before they will marry you. Reform rabbis will perform ceremonies without a get.

Booking the Music

So you love that swing band that played at your cousin's wedding, or you want to have a cool jazz trio perform at your reception. Just remember that at this early stage in the engagement, you also need to book your ceremony music. Sometimes the ceremony music is more of an afterthought. "Oh, yeah, we need music to walk down the aisle to," couples realize. If you want an experienced harpist and pianist, for example, you need to book them in advance as well. You don't necessarily need to hire them as far in advance as the entertainment for your reception (the best bands often book a year in advance). After you sign on for your reception music, you can hire musicians for the ceremony. Would you like an ensemble to play classical music, or a soloist to sing as you saunter down the aisle? If you haven't looked into this yet, ask a wedding band booking agent, wedding coordinator, or your contact at the reception site for names of ceremony musicians.

These instruments are ideal for an elegant ceremony:

- Cello
- Classical guitar
- Flute
- Harp
- Piano

Second-Time Smarts

Have your ceremony musicians relocate to your cocktail area so you have music playing in the background while your guests mingle.

- Viola
- Violin

Small ensembles work well for the ceremony and also for the cocktail hour.

Hiring Your Reception Music

For large, formal, sit-down dinner receptions, bands or orchestras are popular. Usually someone from the band can serve as the master of ceremonies and motivate your guests to get out on the dance floor. Smaller outdoor garden weddings would be an ideal setting for a string quartet or a solo performer (no electricity needed!). But there are no rules for second weddings. You can two-step down the aisle to country and western tunes if you want. Anything goes!

As I already mentioned, the good wedding bands book fast. How fast? Well, when my fiancé and I were happy with a band whose video we saw, we decided to see them perform live at a wedding to make sure they were just as good as their staged performance on tape. The band's manager told us of a wedding they were playing. We got dressed up and peeked inside long enough to see that they were the band for us! We called in the morning to book them and were crushed to hear that another couple beat us to it. The awesome band with the great reputation that got the whole party on the dance floor was going to play at someone else's wedding, not ours.

MICHELE AND ELI'S STORY

I wanted something completely different from my first wedding, which was more traditional, and being almost 10 years older the second time, my taste had changed. We had been to so many weddings that followed the same formula with the attendants, speeches, and bands. We wanted a reception where people would be able to choose where they sat, didn't have to listen to boring speeches, could eat great food in a beautiful surrounding (my in-laws' home), and listen to great music. It was most important to us to book the band. We wanted to use a band that doesn't normally do weddings. The band performs at shows and concerts and we knew our date would be dependent on its availability. We had a world-class jazz band and our 400 guests danced and mingled all night!

When it comes to achieving elegance, my vote is for live music all the way. But if a band isn't in your budget, consider hiring a disc jockey (DJ) for these reasons:

- You won't have some Celine Dion wannabe belting out tunes while adding her own style that doesn't sound at all like your favorite songs.
- Your music genres and sound choices are practically endless, ranging from folk, pop, and reggae to big band and salsa.

Look for a DJ with a great voice and a *mildly* energetic persona. You don't want a completely annoying DJ getting in your guests' faces trying to rally them around the room singing "Hot Hot Hot." You also want a DJ with a vast song collection so he can play your requests as well as your guests' requests. You never want to hear an entertainer say, "Uhh, I don't have that one."

Here is what the American Disc Jockey Association (www.adja.org) advises before hiring a DJ:

Questions to Ask Before Booking Your Music

- What are your rates?
- What kind of deposit is needed to confirm?
- When is the final balance due?
- Have you worked at my reception site before?
- How early will you set up your equipment?
- May I see a video and a live performance of the musicians who will play at my wedding?
- Are you willing to play requests that aren't on your song sheet?
- Do you have a person who serves as an emcee? If so, what are his or her duties?
- What backup plan do you provide if a musician gets sick or has to leave?
- What do the band members or DJ wear?
- How many hours do you play?
- How many breaks do you take?
- How long are your breaks?
- Can we hire you without breaks?
- What are your fees?
- What about overtime fees?
- What are your cancellation and refund policies?

1. Choose a DJ who is registered, incorporated, and/or insured.

2. Check with references about whether your DJ is accessible and happy to meet with you before the wedding.

3. Find out if the DJ uses a professional sound system and what backup plan is offered in case of an equipment problem or any other unforeseen circumstances.

4. Specify how the DJ should dress. You shouldn't have to pay extra if you request a tuxedo.

5. Agree on specific arrival and set-up times.

6. Include a cancellation clause in the contract.

Booking Your Florist

This may go against what you've read or heard before, but I say, book your florist early. Some wedding industry folks will say that the florist can wait because a florist can take on several weddings a day but a band, for example, can be at only one location at a time. For some brides, it's safe to assume that the lower the florist is on the priority list, the likelier it is that any florist will do. Many first-time brides don't know what kind of flowers they want, or they may be at the mercy of their mother's choice of florist, or they may have the attitude that a rose is a rose and anyone can handle a wedding. But second-time brides often have a clearer idea of what they want, and flowers are a big part of the wedding.

You know that not all florists are the best. Some may be great for ordering a generic Mother's Day arrangement, but they don't have the staff to personally assist you or the design talent to create the unique look you want. You wouldn't bother with a florist who isn't on-site to see that the décor is executed. You wouldn't risk handing over your precious day to a mass merchant who is handling 20 other weddings that day. You want your wedding to be a

Second-Time Smarts

To find a disc jockey on the Internet, contact the American Disc Jockey Association at www.adja.org or check out the Web site, www .proDJ.com.

priority. You want someone who will take the time to order your specific floral colors in advance and who will scout out the necessary props such as vases and pedestals.

For Tim Hourigan of The Flower Company in Royal Oak, Michigan, 30 percent of his business is second weddings. "Eighty percent of my brides book the church, the hall, and then the florist," he says. "We only take three weddings a day, but some florists will take 15 weddings a day. We get brides who come to us before they get their dress. They are familiar with our work, and some book a year in advance."

Even if you are 100 percent set on which florist you want, it's still a good idea to interview a couple of others. When meeting with florists, be honest about your budget so they can advise you on how to create elegance without going beyond your means. You will at least find out whether you are being charged fairly. If nothing else, meeting others and seeing samples of their work can make you feel even better about the florist you're leaning toward.

Professionally Speaking

Flowers seem to become more of a priority to second-time brides. They want lush, beautiful flowers and usually have strong opinions and have developed their style. They are more relaxed than first-time brides, easy to deal with, and they seem more trusting of the vendors.

—Sayles Livingston, Sayles Livingston Flowers

Where I'm from, the florist is always one of the top vendors to book. As soon as people are asking to see your ring and whether you picked a date, they are asking who's doing your flowers. Many brides will want to work with only a certain florist because that is the person who best understands their vision and how to execute it. Many florists not only design your flowers but also provide the rentals and set up the room from linens to lanterns. Sayles Livingston, owner of Sayles Livingston Flowers (www.sayleslivingston flowers.com) in Adamsville, Rhode island, is selective about the number of events she takes on in one weekend because she designs and creates all the flower arrangements herself and she personally selects all the flowers she uses.

Professionally Speaking

I would ask your florist about time commitments for your wedding date. If you are looking for only a delivery of flowers, then most florists would be able to accommodate your order. If they have more than one commitment on that particular day, you would need to set aside more service time from your florist, and maybe even expect to pay a service fee for the actual time they commit; for example, pinning on the corsages or boutonnieres.

—Lynne Moss, president-elect of the American Institute of Floral Designers

What to Look For

Look for someone who will help you express your personality. Make sure you review their portfolio to see if you like their style. If you want to be creative and have wild arrangements, make sure your florist has practice stepping out of the box. If every picture in the portfolio shows the same uniform look of roses on each table, he or she isn't the most original.

Kristy Eidam, consumer marketing manager at the Society of American Florists (SAF) in Alexandria, Virginia, offers these tips:

• Look for a florist who is affiliated with a professional group: national wire services such as FTD and Teleflora; national trade associations such as SAF; industry organizations such as the American Institute of Floral Designers (AIFD); and state and local trade associations.

• Book the florist six months to a year in advance for a wedding during peak wedding season or on a holiday, or if you want something really elaborate.

• Provide the florist with information. Bring pictures of flowers you like, a photo of your dress, or a swatch of fabric. If you know

Questions to Ask Before Booking Your Florist

- What services do you provide?

- Can I see pictures of your designs?

- What are your rates?

- What kinds of extras are not included?

- On what items is there a sales tax?

- How many weddings do you handle in a weekend? In a day?

- How many weddings have you done?

- Have you done any second weddings?

- Have you done any weddings at our location?

- How many weddings do you have on our date?

- How early will you arrive to set up?

- What kind of deposit is needed to confirm?

- When is the final balance due?

- Will you create the arrangements, or will your staffers?

- Do you rent items such as linens and props?

- Do you deliver? If so, what do you charge?

- What are your cancellation and refund policies?

what type of wedding you want, the florist can start suggesting possible flowers.

Many industry experts advise bringing a plethora of information to the florist interview, from the material of the gowns to the colors you want to play up. It's great if you can offer that information, but if you still aren't sure what colors you want, whether you want a theme, or which kinds of flowers would work best for your location, that's fine. You're just booking the florist. You don't have to commit to exact colors and combinations quite yet. That will come in time—you may want to work with your florist in dreaming up the perfect floral display, or you may be completely open to running with one of his or her ideas.

Booking Your Photographer

If it's been several years since your first wedding, you will be surprised by the changes in wedding photography. The standard was always the traditional photographer, but now another wave of wedding photography has become popular—photojournalism. It really took off when a certain celebrity wedding picture hit the media. Who can forget John F. Kennedy Jr. sweetly kissing his bride Carolyn Bessette Kennedy's hand as they walked down the chapel steps? It was a candid moment taken by society and celebrity photographer Denis Reggie.

Second-Time Smarts

Decide what you want by checking out different flowers by name and picture. The Society of American Florists offers a great resource on the Internet at www.aboutflowers.com.

Almost immediately, brides weren't interested in a backdrop behind them while a photographer staged their posed pictures. They wanted a more natural approach, nothing forced. With this documentary style, the photographer—an unobtrusive (imagine that) bystander—is following the action and capturing the play-by-play of beautiful, tender moments of your wedding. You should have no problem finding a photographer who offers this approach.

The elders in your family may want some traditional portraits. In that case, ask the photographer to do a little of both styles.

You want your wedding pictures to be around forever. You'll pass them down to future generations. I love pictures and have them all over my home, and you could bet I wasn't going to hire

Questions to Ask Before Booking Your Photographer

- What is your style—traditional portraits, photojournalism, a mix of both?
- Do you use natural light?
- What kinds of packages do you have?
- What are your fees?
- Have you worked at my reception site before?
- How many rolls of film do you shoot?
- How many hours do you usually work at a wedding like ours?
- Are there any extra charges?
- When should we expect to receive the proofs? What about the finished albums?
- Do you work with an assistant?
- Can you take black-and-white and color shots?
- May we take the proofs home to view?
- Will you let us keep the proofs?
- What kind of deposit is needed to confirm?
- What is your backup plan and who is the photographer in case of an emergency or cancellation?
- What do you wear to shoot weddings?
- When is the final balance due?
- What are your cancellation and refund policies?

just any photographer who happened to be available on my wedding day. I did my research and found someone in my area who specialized in photojournalism. I saw samples of his work and was impressed.

Even if you've looked through your friends' wedding albums, have a clear idea of what you do and don't want, and are already considering a photographer, it's still a good idea to meet with a few other photographers so you can compare what they offer. Ask to meet with the person who would actually be photographing your wedding.

Candid pictures can be in black and white or color. Black-and-white photos are timeless and sophisticated but they may cost more because the film is usually more expensive to process. Hand-colored, digital, infrared, or sepia photos offer other interesting approaches.

Several photographers I researched before my second wedding claimed that they took photojournalistic black-and-white pictures. What they really did was take their color shots and had them printed on black-and-white paper. Guess what? It's not the same thing. The quality of the photos is not the same. The pictures aren't as sharp.

If the documentary-style photography interests you, ask where your photographer was trained in photojournalism. If he or she has been specializing in traditional, posed shots for 25 years, how did he or she suddenly get the experience of capturing moments from behind the scenes, as they happen?

I was recently at a wedding where the photographer lined everyone up like soldiers for each picture. He told us when to

Professionally Speaking

Good photojournalists/documentary photographers usually have traditionally based techniques in mind when they search for candid moments. They usually understand lighting, composition, and facial analysis, and they know where to be and when to be there.

—Lauran Wycoff of Lauran Wycoff Photography in Scottsdale, Arizona smile, turn, lean, and wave. I felt like I needed permission to breathe. Then, to make matters worse, he'd run back to his camera and wave his hand in the air making silly smiling faces as if we were three-year-olds waiting for the cue to smile with Santa. It was dreadful. But you can spare yourself such annoyances by booking the type of photographer you feel most comfortable with and whose work really impresses you. Remember, the night may fly by but your pictures are forever.

Contract Checklist

You may have your own contract "musts," but here is a basic guide worth reviewing before you sign a contract:

- ❑ Your name and all correct contact information
- ❑ Name of the vendor or site
- ❑ Vendor's contact information: phone, pager, cellular, and e-mail
- ❑ Exactly what or who you are getting and the exact time of service from start to end
- ❑ Date, time, and location (specifically the room or area of the grounds where the wedding will be)
- ❑ All fees
- ❑ Overtime fees
- ❑ Deposit information
- ❑ Payment information
- ❑ Cancellation information
- ❑ Backup plan in writing if they should cancel. Will they line up a replacement?
- ❑ Vendor's signature

When Vendors Think They're All That–Dealing with Attitude

It isn't enough that vendors just answer your questions. Make sure you also get a positive vibe from the people you hire. While you're shopping around, notice how the vendors treat you. Are they happy to answer your questions, or do they seem annoyed that you are asking so many? Do they seem willing to hear your ideas? Can you picture working closely with them or trusting them to help make your wedding beautiful? Are you comfortable with them, or do they rub you the wrong way?

Often, you won't deal directly with the florist or band until your scheduled appointments. You may have to talk to their assistants, managers, or associates. If the help is rude to you, you can always take your business elsewhere. One bride hired a florist who was supposed to be the best in town. His staff was so rude to her when she went to visit the shop that she found another florist.

Second-Time Discrimination?

Encore brides shouldn't receive attitude just because it's not their first time, says Bonnie Graham, creator and producer of Second Wedding Showcase, Inc. (www.secondweddingshowcase.com), a special events company that offers advice, ideas, and vendors to encore brides. Graham also coordinates second-wedding bridal expos. "The main reason I did the showcase is because second-time brides aren't always treated well at the first-time-blushing-bride expos," she says. "Perhaps some vendors assume that brides in their thirties don't have as big a budget as brides whose parents are paying." The message Graham wants to give brides is that they deserve both another chance at happiness, and the resources to help them plan a beautiful second wedding.

Avoid the vendor who seems to be interviewing you to find out if your wedding will be worthwhile enough for him to take on. There are vendors who want to handle only society weddings within a certain price range. If they give you attitude, walk out. It's not worth being miserable because you can't stand your florist. There is plenty of amazing talent you can work with—let it be the snooty vendor's loss.

You're getting closer to your big day, and you've booked your big five. Doesn't it feel good? You're only going to feel better as your wedding approaches!

Legally Speaking

What You Need to Know from Changing Your Name to Prenuptial Agreements

Before we dive into wedding wonder, let's get the paper pushing over with. The county courthouse staffers won't just take your word for it when you tell them you're divorced. You will need your divorce papers to prove that you are in fact divorced before you can legally get married. If you are a widow, you will need your husband's death certificate.

Marriage Licenses

As you know, you need a marriage license to make your marriage legal. You need to check with the marriage-license bureau or the county clerk's office in your area—and possibly also where your wedding will be held—to find out about the marriage laws. They vary by county and state. Find out which blood tests are required before you can get your license and when you should apply. Be sure to bring the required paperwork. You'll also need a certified birth certificate, driver's license, or state photo ID.

Prenuptial Agreements

Prenuptial agreements (prenups) are contracts executed before marriage, detailing the division of your marital assets, debts, and obligations should you get divorced. Not the most romantic notion to discuss in the beginning of your engagement, I know, but for some, it's necessary.

Brides-to-be don't often joyfully plan a prenup. You haven't even booked the caterer yet and already I'm talking about life's "what ifs" such as divorce. What nerve! So why am I bringing up such a serious topic? Well, the fact is, prenuptial agreements are more common in second marriages than in first marriages. I also bring up the "P" word because if you have children, you may see a prenuptial agreement as something to do for their sake. It's not a likely topic in first-time-bride books, but it's worth exploring prior to a second trip down the aisle.

Some of the most popular questions asked by second-time brides-to-be are about prenuptial agreements. For example:

- Should I ask my fiancé to sign a prenup?
- Why would I need a prenup?
- Do we need separate lawyers?
- How do I bring up the subject?

Perhaps it never even occurred to you to draw up a prenuptial agreement the first time you got married, but now that you have experienced divorce or widowhood, you'll consider looking into it. Older and wiser, you are entering your second marriage with more than a college degree or the clothes on your back. This time, you may have children, a business, a home, retirement funds, and assets ranging from jewelry to art and antiques. It's not that you don't believe in love, it's just that you want to protect your children or assets no matter what.

I've heard stories of couples who called off their engagement because one of them didn't want to sign a prenuptial agreement. Some were horrified just being asked. "It's puzzling and disappointing that prenups have such a bad rap, considering how effective they can be in promoting a healthier marriage and, if they're ever needed, saving everyone time, grief, and money," says Carrie Coghill, certified financial planner, president of D. B. Root & Company Financial Planning in Pittsburgh, Pennsylvania, and author of *The Newlyweds' Guide to Investing & Personal Finance.*

Second-time brides face many of the same challenges as first-time newlyweds, but the details (ex-spouses, separate homes, kids) are usually more complicated. That's why communication is even more important in second marriages. Whether or not you feel that a prenuptial agreement is right for you, don't wait until after you are married to address your financial issues as a couple. Will you stay home to raise the kids? Is your fiancé willing to take care of your elderly parents down the road? These can turn into hot topics once you are married, so start talking now.

Second-Time Smarts

If you are not sure about whether or not you want a prenuptial agreement, you might want to talk to a lawyer for more information. The Web site www.lawyers.com offers a free database of 440,000 attorneys searchable by location and specialty.

Many marital problems revolve around money, and if you are upfront about your finances and financial plans, you will have already jumped one hurdle. "When couples have a prenup, they tend to worry and fight less over money because they have the security of already communicating about these difficult issues," says Coghill.

Who Wants a Prenup?

Possible scenarios that might warrant a prenuptial agreement:

- You have children. Wanting to protect your kids' inheritance rights is the most popular reason for prenups, which can facilitate the distribution of assets if a spouse dies.

- You are financially independent. If you are bringing your income, mutual funds, and pricey toys into the marriage, you can put in writing which assets were pre-marital.

- If you're part of a family business, a prenup could protect the business should your marital status change.

- You are inheriting money. A prenup can protect the inheritance from landing in a possible ex-in-law's hands.

Alan Kopit, a partner at Cleveland-based law firm Hahn Loeser & Parks LLP, legal advisor for lawyers.com, and regular legal contributor to NBC-TV's *Today* show, says that if you are getting married for the second time—particularly if you have children—you should seriously consider a prenuptial agreement. "You really need to think about how your children are going to be protected if the second marriage ends with a death or divorce," he says.

You Want Me to What?

If you've decided you want a prenuptial agreement, now comes the tough part. How do you bring up the subject without sending your fiancé running out the door? What may seem like a smart financial move for you may completely offend your honey. He may think you don't trust him or that you are inferring that he's a gold digger. You'll have to handle this one with care.

Patricia Schiff Estess, author of *Money Advice for Your Successful Remarriage,* says second-time brides should have prenuptial talks.

She says a possible opener could be: "We both know from experience how money can be a source of conflict in a marriage. . . . I'd feel much better if we could talk openly about it now. . . . I'd feel more comfortable if we could agree on some possible sticking

America on Prenups

When you hear the word *prenup,* are you thinking either (a) old, (b) rich, or (c) famous? That's not surprising, since 25 percent of Americans think prenups aren't for "regular" people. One in five believes that a prenup is never needed if two people really love each other, and another 15 percent are convinced that a prenup dooms a marriage to fail. If you want to know more about Americans' attitudes toward prenups, check out these results from a recent survey conducted by Harris Interactive for lawyers.com:

• Twenty-eight percent of Americans say that prenups make smart financial sense for anyone getting married.

• Seventy-nine percent of Americans see some benefit to having a prenup.

• Unmarried women older than age 55 are more likely than any other demographic group to demand a prenuptial agreement before getting married. They are interested in protecting assets they bring into the marriage or money they earn during the marriage.

• Divorced Americans are more supportive of prenups than those who have never been married: 17 percent of all divorced Americans say they would never remarry without one; only 6 percent of never-married Americans say they would require a prenup before they'd tie the knot.

• Thirty-four percent of men between ages 18 and 34 think prenups are a smart financial move, but 22 percent of men in that age range would be too uncomfortable bringing up the subject in their own relationships. Only 11 percent of women the same age say they would feel too uncomfortable to discuss prenups in their relationships.

Second-Time Smarts

My fiancé and I think a prenuptial agreement is a good idea. Although neither of us are independently wealthy, I am self-employed and I am developing another business. I actually approached him about the subject. I said, "You know how awful my divorce was, would you mind doing this for me so I don't have to worry about it?" My fiancé understands because he's been through a divorce before, too. It also helps that he has an innate sense of fairness and that we have an established pattern of keeping our money separate and contributing to a joint account for our joint expenditures. We just want to take precautions.

—Shannon

points and put them on paper in some sort of prenuptial agreement. What do you think?"

Estess also suggests:

- Drawing up a will before your wedding.
- Making sure you understand a prenuptial agreement's ramifications completely before you sign.
- Seeing that the agreement is fair and protects you.
- Finding out what you're entitled to under the laws in your state if your future marriage ends in divorce or death.
- Never signing a prenup if you're feeling pressured.

Prenups are not just for the old and rich. Kopit says second-timers in their 20s and 30s need to consider them if their current situation may change. You may think, "Heck, we aren't worth zilch," but just because you don't own a house or a car today doesn't mean you won't in the future. Your assets could change 5 or 10 years from now. You may start a successful business or buy property, and a prenup can address how you are going to deal with the changes. If a hefty inheritance is headed your way a few years from now, what would happen to it if you got divorced?

Be prepared when you meet with your attorney about a prenuptial agreement. You and your fiancé should make a detailed list of your assets, liabilities, income, alimony, child support, life insurance, and business interests, and should provide past tax returns. Before signing a prenuptial agreement, know that full disclosure is essential—without it the agreement may be challenged and become null and void.

Things you may not know about prenups:

- The terms and issues are flexible.
- You can put just about anything you want in a prenup so long as it is legal and does not violate public policy.
- Prenups can be modified or terminated at any time if both parties agree.
- Prenups can be challenged in a court of law.
- Prenups should be updated once you've been married for a while, or after an important life change such as a new baby or serious illness.
- You and your fiancé need separate legal representation for a prenup.

Professionally Speaking

People think that prenuptial agreements are for the man protecting his assets from his second wife in case they get divorced. That is a small aspect. If you have a child, you need to provide for your child and make sure you are not leaving everything to your spouse. A prenuptial agreement is a good idea. Anyone can get in an accident at any time. If you haven't protected your children, then you haven't done your job as a parent.
—Beth Reed Ramirez, editor of *Bride Again,* an online magazine for women planning to remarry

Changing Your Name

In the midst of your engagement excitement, you have to decide whether or not to change your name. And if you do, what will be your game plan? Will you do it right away? Will you slowly allow yourself time to get used to it? Will you add his name to your last name and later drop your current last name? Will you hyphenate?

Should I Do It—Again?

This is a sticky topic. Many women lament over the thought of having to change their name—again. The name-changing question is difficult to answer, especially when you have kids. People can get confused when you have a different last name than your children. Often the kids want to keep their father's last name, unless your fiancé is adopting them. Some women choose to stick with their first husband's name because that is how people know them. And then there are women who never changed their last name to begin with. If there are children, there will be three different last names in the family.

I agonized over what to do about changing my name. I remember sitting in the courtroom when I got divorced, waiting to legally get my maiden name back. When it was official, I felt liberated and I vowed to never change my name again. So then two name changes behind me, a few different bylines for work, what do I do? I fall in love with my husband, Bobby, and I contemplate the whole name change thing all over again.

I knew I wanted to take Bobby's name in my personal life because when we eventually had kids, I wanted to have the same last name as they did. I figured I could keep my maiden name professionally. My dual-name system worked for a while, but when I was speaking with people I'd always have to remember which

Wedding Day Reflections

I really did not want to change my name after my second wedding (even though I did the first time I got married) because I was building my professional reputation. But my husband is a traditional guy and I knew it would bother him if I didn't. We talked about it and I eventually hyphenated instead, which really bugs everyone! Hyphenation is what happens when a feminist marries a traditionalist.

—Kelly

name they knew. Sometimes I'd leave voicemail messages giving my married name, when they knew me by my maiden name. So ultimately I took the plunge—again—and made my husband's name my third name. Although it probably makes Dad happy that I proudly carry on his family name, I'm not sure how Mom feels about my relinquishing my given middle name, Lynn. Professionally I'm known now as Julie Weingarden Dubin. It's a mouthful, but it's who I am. I get mail addressed to several different names. And for a while, my purse contained credit cards with three different last names. Oh, the things we do for love!

Making the Change

Before you change your name, be sure your identification (driver's license and passport) will reflect the name on your honeymoon tickets. If you booked your tickets with your maiden name, you'll have to wait until after you return from your trip to change your name officially. The last thing you want is for security to detain you at the airport because they don't believe you are really you.

In order to be recognized officially by your new name, you need to go to the Social Security office in your area and fill out the proper forms. At this time you'll also officially change your marital status, if you are already married. But don't put down your pen just yet. You have more forms to fill out.

Your family and friends will want to know whether or not you are changing your name. You can just send out an announcement similar to a new-address card. I have friends who did not take their husband's name, and they get annoyed when family members address invitations to Mr. and Mrs. Smith, for example. You also need to notify your colleagues, children's schools, family doctors and dentists, credit card companies, health/car/life insurance companies, banks, and car leasing companies. Remember to update everything from your stocks and bonds to your magazine subscriptions.

You'll need to change all of these:

- Social Security card
- Passport
- Driver's license
- Car registration
- Voter registration card
- Work identification card
- Fitness club card
- Bank cash card

And while you're at it, contact these places:

- Post office
- Mortgage company
- Phone company
- Personnel office at work
- Cable company

In addition to contacting people by mail, be sure to change your name on your voice mail at work or home. You may even want to get a new e-mail address to reflect your new name. While you're at it, you might want to order new checks, stationery, and address labels, so they are ready when you get back from your honeymoon. Go ahead and let the world know you're getting married!

You Do!

PLANNING YOUR CEREMONY

At second weddings, every little aspect seems to have more significance. Brides tell me they do more research about the meaning behind things, such as what certain flowers or colors signify. Many brides didn't have the time or desire to do such research prior to their first wedding because they were simply overwhelmed with bridal duties.

As most second-timers will tell you, the ceremony is the most important part of the wedding (though you wouldn't know it by the way some brides-to-be turn planning a wedding reception into a full-time job). Maybe they didn't put much thought into it at their first wedding, but many brides tell me their second marriage ceremonies were truly meaningful and beautiful. "You could feel the love in the room," says one bride. "I'll never forget how close I felt to him during those moments," says another.

Whether you see yourself as a traditional bride walking down the church aisle with Dad, or as an alternative bride getting hitched at a midnight campfire with friends singing Enya songs in the background, you can do whatever pleases you. There are no rules. You are not limited. Your ceremony can be every bit as enriching and rewarding as you hope it will be. You don't have to just quietly run through the motions with a small ceremony. Be true to your heart and your relationship and plan a ceremony that will be fulfilling and memorable for both of you.

Religious or Civil Ceremony?

You do not have to abandon your faith just because you're getting married for the second time. You *can* have a religious ceremony; you just have to check with your officiant or place of worship to find out what requirements you must meet before they can marry you. For example, do you need to participate in premarital counseling? Do you need to meet with the religious officiant for a few "getting-to-know-you" sessions? Do you have to show any paperwork such as baptism and confirmation records or a "get" (Jewish divorce document)?

If your parents insisted on the officiant or the type of ceremony for your first wedding, this is an opportunity to have the ceremony you and your groom both want. Selecting an officiant together can be a wonderful bonding experience.

Civil Ceremonies

A civil ceremony doesn't have to mean exchanging vows in a tiny, sterile city hall. You may choose to have a lovely, intimate ceremony in a judge's chambers, or you may want a larger ceremony on a country club terrace. You have many options; just make sure the public officiant of your choice will travel. Not all public officiants will work outside of their offices or after business hours, so find out what their limits are before you hire them. If you want to personalize the civil ceremony by adding your own thoughts or reading passages from your favorite poem or reciting the lyrics to the song you both feel epitomizes your relationship, just be sure the officiant is open to tweaking his or her usual ceremony.

> ## Second-Time Smarts
>
> Be sure to allow for a longer engagement if either of you plan on converting. You'll need time to go through the necessary conversion classes. Some religions require a significant amount of study before you can convert.

Depending on where you are getting married, your civil ceremony may be performed by various public officiants, such as a magistrate, justice of the peace, mayor, or governor.

Can a Bosom Buddy Marry You Like Joey on *Friends?*

Some states will issue a special license to allow a friend or family member to be an officiant for the day so someone close to you can perform your ceremony. Check with the laws of the state where the wedding will take place. It's a great honor to bestow on someone, but make sure they are up to the task—that they are willing to show up early, be on time for the rehearsal, and perform the ceremony according to your request. You don't want your actor friend to make the ceremony all about himself because he just likes hearing himself talk. The person you choose will likely be someone dear to both you and your groom. If he or she wants to throw in a few good wishes, make sure you know beforehand what he or she will share in front of all your guests.

Marla and Jeff decided to do something original for their ceremony. Because he is Catholic and she is Jewish, finding a perfect solution to who would marry them was a challenge. They ended up asking a special friend to become ordained on the Internet and perform the ceremony. They wrote their own vows and incorporated readings from family and friends. Marla's six-year-old daughter took part in the beach ceremony, which was also attended by Jeff's cocker spaniel.

Interfaith Issues

If you want to know how to incorporate your separate religions into your ceremony, ask other couples how they did it, and specifically ask which rituals were included. You may want to watch a video or DVD of other interfaith ceremonies to see what you do or don't want.

If you and your fiancé plan to include elements of both of your religions in your ceremony, be sure to check with your officiants before you hire them to make sure they are willing to perform the ceremony together. For example, if you are hiring a rabbi and minister, ask them if they are willing to work together. Some officiants are used to taking the lead, and that might result in a ceremony that isn't balanced enough for you and your fiancé.

Can Your Folks Escort You Down the Aisle?

You can have your pick of people or pets to walk you down the aisle. Some second-time brides choose to walk alone, while others walk in with their children or their groom. It's perfectly acceptable for you to walk down the aisle with one or both parents or meet them halfway. Your parents are still your parents, whether or not you're a first-time bride. You can have a son, daughter, friend, brother, sister, aunt, uncle—whomever you want to walk you down the aisle. It's your day.

Personalizing Your Ceremony

Whether your ceremony is big or small, religious or civil, the one common link in second weddings is the attention paid to detail. The ceremony is a top priority, and couples want theirs to be personalized—a ceremony that will speak to them. They want more than a generic fill-in-the-blank presentation.

I loved my second wedding ceremony. I remember my husband's arm around my lower back, holding me close as the rabbi spoke about our relationship and the qualities we cherish in one another. Our hands were entwined as we stood under the chuppah listening to the cantor's angelic voice serenade us in Hebrew. At one point during the music, we leaned our heads together and closed our eyes as we just took in the beautiful melody and magic of the moment.

We wrote and read our own vows to each other and then we recited some vows together. I listened to every word. Our rabbi met with us several times before

Wedding Day Reflections

My first wedding was a religious service to please my parents. At my second wedding, a mayor performed our ceremony. She had a set service but she allowed us to make any additions or subtractions as we saw fit. She gave us several options when it came to the wording—some were more traditional ("I promise to love, honor, obey . . .) and others were more romantic ("I promise to be true to you, to believe in you . . ."). My husband stepped on the glass at the end to honor my Jewish heritage, and we lit the unity candle to honor his Christian heritage. It was short and simple while at the same time being warm and loving.

–Leslie

She's Got Personality

Beth Reed Ramirez, editor of *Bride Again*, an online publication for women planning to remarry, arrived at her country club golf course ceremony in a red golf cart driven by her dad. The setting was perfect for the bride and groom, both of whom are golf lovers. The duo added another surprise twist to their ceremony: When the pastor asked the groom if he'd take Beth to be his bride, music from the TV show *Jeopardy* started playing. "My husband watches *Jeopardy* every single night. We don't even eat dinner until after 7:30 P.M.," she says. "Humor is part of our life and marriage, and we wanted to incorporate that into our ceremony."

our wedding and wanted to learn about our relationship—the good and the bad. He asked what was special about the other person and he listened to our concerns. He was respectful of what we wanted to include in our ceremony. He was personable and added humor and warmth to the ceremony. I felt that our ceremony was like no one else's.

Words of Love

A great way to personalize your ceremony is to write your own vows. When you vow your love to each other before family and friends, why not exchange your own words—words that have meaning to you? Whether romantic, clever, serious, or funny, all that matters is that your vows are from the heart. (You can read more about writing your own vows in chapter 17.) If you choose to repeat the traditional vows, you can still add special elements that reflect you and your groom. Perhaps the rabbi, priest, minister, or judge will talk about how you met, or about the recent obstacle you moved past, or even about your hopes and dreams for the future.

You may find yourself faced with an officiant who has a certain way of leading marriage ceremonies. If you feel you are not being heard, speak up. Don't let the officiant take control of your ceremony. Express to him or her what you want your ceremony to be like, who you want to give readings or stand beside you.

Once you decide on the type of ceremony you want, be sure to meet with your officiant as the date approaches so he or she can go over the ceremony and describe what will happen so you are not clueless about what comes next. You may get a sheet of certain prayers or phrases so you can become familiar with them or even practice. Your officiant will also let you know when it will be time for you and your groom to turn to one another and recite your vows.

Writing your own vows and committing them to memory is great. But it's wise to have them written down on index cards— just in case. After all, no one wants to go blank and be vowless. Your groom should be speechless only when he sees you walk down the aisle! For our ceremony, the rabbi handed us our cards, and that was our cue to exchange vows. There was no pressure to try to remember the order of the words. Our ceremony flowed.

Let the Music Play

Second-time couples often like to personalize their ceremony with music that reflects their relationship. Not many first-time brides feel comfortable telling Mom and the church organist to forgo standards such as the "Wedding March" or "Ave Maria" in favor of songs by The Rolling Stones or U2. But in second weddings, music is often an important way of expressing your love and how far you've come in your relationship. "I carefully picked out our songs so they were meaningful, special, and unique," says Lauran, a

30-year-old second-time bride. "My processional song will be Prince's 'The Most Beautiful Girl in the World.' I'm a huge Prince fan and it's a beautiful song." Jessica, also 30, chose to walk down the aisle to "My Best Friend," by Queen, and selected "So Happy Together" by the Turtles for the bridal party's entrance.

SUZY AND STEPHEN'S STORY

I was 32 at my first wedding and 44 at my second wedding. I had 190 guests at my first wedding and 210 guests at my second wedding. Our ceremony was personal and beautiful. It was a true joining of two families. Our nieces and nephews walked down the aisle, our aunts and uncles held the chuppah poles, our cousins said the seven blessings, our siblings were our attendants, and our parents walked us down the aisle. Touching words were said during the ceremony about my husband's father, who died in 1997. It also had creative elements. My husband, who is a big tennis player, brought his creativity into the ceremony. Our nephews walked down the aisle with tennis rackets slung over their shoulders, the ring pillows had oversized tennis balls glued to the tops, and at the end of the ceremony two canisters filled with rose petals exploded and shot petals into the air.

For Carolyn, 38, the second wedding was the flip side of the first, which was a traditional church wedding with a choir and full mass. Her second wedding featured an outdoor interfaith ceremony. "Instead of the church organ we had a Spanish guitarist playing during the ceremony," she says. "He was the guitarist at the restaurant where we had our first date. We tried to include people from our courtship in our wedding."

Cultural Traditions

Sometimes second-time couples take an interest in their heritage or choose to honor cultural traditions. Perhaps the groom will wear a kilt to honor his Scottish heritage, which he didn't feel comfortable doing at his first wedding. Maybe you'll have someone sing an Irish song that your grandmother loved, or you'll walk down the aisle to a beautiful Spanish melody rather than the traditional wedding song.

Or how about creating a new ritual or tradition in your family? You can be as creative as you want. Maybe your siblings will add this element to their weddings, too. If you have children, your ceremony is an opportunity to celebrate your relationship with your husband-to-be and their relationship to their stepfather-to-be. If you are marrying a man with children, you want to publicly commit to them as well. It's important for children to feel that they are becoming part of something greater rather than being left behind. Your children can participate in the ceremony in many ways, from standing by your side to escorting you down the aisle or serenading you. (You can read more about getting your children involved in chapter 20.)

> ## Wedding Day Reflections
>
> We wanted to honor our heritage, so we had the seats in the second row decorated with flowers and rose petals so that they were "reserved" for our ancestors to be with us that day.
> —Christine

LAURAN'S STORY

I'll have a small bouquet of roses when I make my entrance, and as I walk down the aisle I'll collect 18 other roses from special people in our lives. When I get to the end of the aisle, my mother will tie a satin bow around the roses. We're having two readings, one by my fiancé's 10-year-old son and the other by a good friend of mine. My fiancé's two daughters and two sons will light the unity candle with us so that it will be a family lighting, uniting all of us together. We are writing our own vows and I hope I'll be able to convince my fiancé to let our dog be the flower girl!

———————————

Remembering Loved Ones

One of the greatest things about being a second-time bride is being able to change the things you didn't like about your first wedding. With your been-there-done-that wisdom, you know what you

Personal Touches

- Honor deceased loved ones with framed photos and a rose before each one, on a table at the ceremony entrance.

- Ask the people who fixed you up to read a special poem.

- Arrange for your attendants to walk down the aisle with objects that represent your interests or relationship.

- Create a little program explaining the meaning behind the different elements of your ceremony, and briefly describe how you and your groom met or what you love about one another.

- Let your little ones sing a special song as they walk down the aisle instead of having them walk to classical music.

- Give your dog the honor of walking down the aisle sporting a bow tie, or wheel "Sparky" down the aisle in a wagon decorated with flowers.

want to do differently. But I must say there are things I wish I would have done differently at my second wedding, too. Looking back, there will always be something you're going to wish you could change, no matter how perfectly you put your plans in motion. The stars could all be aligned on your wedding night, but still something may go wrong.

I absolutely loved our ceremony, but in hindsight, I wish we had done something to honor our deceased grandparents. I grew up extremely close to all four of my grandparents, and when I got married, my two grandfathers were no longer with us. A mention, a prayer, or a reading for Bobby's two grandmothers, two grandfathers, and my two grandfathers would have been perfect. But I didn't think about it until afterward. I've since heard beautiful ways of honoring special loved ones. You can leave an empty spot or chair for a friend who died. You can light an altar candle in memory of a parent.

The Sticky Question of Divorced or Remarried Parents

When family members who normally want nothing to do with one another have to appear together because they love you and want to support you, it can make for a rather stressful wedding weekend. If either set of parents has divorced or remarried, it adds another element to the ceremony setup. What if you are having a Christian ceremony and you want your stepfather to walk you down the aisle because you are close to him? What do you do with your father? If your parents or your fiancé's parents are divorced, do you still seat them together in the front row? In a Jewish ceremony, which parents get to stand under the chuppah?

In an ideal world, all the exes and their partners would get along and you could plan your ceremony as you see fit. But if there is tension or a strong dislike among the parents and/or stepparents, you are probably going to take them into consideration. In the end, it will give you less to worry about. My husband's parents are divorced, and he wanted both his mother and his father to meet him at the end of the aisle and walk with him up to the chuppah. They stood under the chuppah side by side. Everything worked out beautifully. His mother was escorted down the aisle by my husband's brothers; then his father walked down the aisle with his wife, and she took her seat in the first row. Everyone involved felt honored by their role in the ceremony. In a Christian ceremony, you can seat divorced parents in the same row, but you may want to place some buffer family members between them. If any parents are remarried, let them sit with their spouses.

Although you may want to avoid the topic of telling your immediate family where they are supposed to sit or stand, it's actually helpful if you express your wishes early on. If you explain what you want, they'll have time to get used to the idea of standing one foot away from the ex they haven't seen in six years. They will realize it's important to you to be surrounded by your family. Come right out and ask your parents if they can put aside their differences for one night.

If you are really stressed out about how to handle the various sets of parents, hire a wedding coordinator just for a half-day to set up the ceremony, and let her deal with the headaches and the family feuds. The ceremony will fly by anyway and they can enjoy the rest of the wedding surrounded by whomever they want.

If worse comes to worse, the feuding family members will just have to learn to tolerate each other—at least temporarily. Don't

Wedding Day Reflections

We didn't have attendants at our ceremony, we just had all of our friends and family standing in a circle around us. My dad had died, so my mom and I walked in together. My husband's mom had died, so he walked in with his dad and stepmom. I loved the warmth of making everyone a part of our ceremony instead of being up on stage feeling like we were performing.

—Beth

worry about it. Your job is to smile and have fun. Try not to let the tension get to you. Remember, this day isn't about them—it's all about you and your groom!

While you're making your plans, be open and honest about your wishes and you'll have your dream ceremony. I recently watched our wedding video to check out my post-ceremony demeanor, and here's what I said: "The ceremony was beautiful—beyond anything I could have dreamed of. I just felt as though life was perfect while I was standing under the chuppah with Bobby and our nearest and dearest. It was just the warmest and most special time of my life."

I know your ceremony also will be magical. And at the other end of the aisle, a new beginning awaits!

Don't Forget the Groom

How to Divvy Up the Duties and Share the Fun

You're probably thinking this is a chapter you don't see in beginner-bride books. But let's be frank—are grooms even taken into account in first weddings? One of my friends recalls that he attended the tasting for his wedding reception and realized that for him it just meant "free food," but for his mother-in-law-to-be, it was actually a "tasting." He didn't get a vote. It didn't matter that the salad tasted awful. It looked pretty. He realized that his job as the groom was to just shut up and eat.

When the bride-to-be is being dragged all over town from appointment to appointment with Mom, where is the groom? In many cases, he's:

A) At work (anything to get out of meeting with the wedding coordinator).

B) At home watching TV and not answering the phone because he really doesn't want to hear you stress about which pattern of china to pick.

C) At the gym trying to get rid of the "I've become comfortable in my relationship" flab for his walk down the aisle.

D) At the bar with his buddies looking at all the cocktail wait-
resses he'll never have.

The twenty-something first-time groom looks forward to his
bachelor party. He made it through the hard part—the proposal
and picking out and paying for the perfect ring. Now he's thinking
he just has to rent a tux and show up come W-Day.

But if you were assuming that your second-time-around fiancé
will take a backseat to your plans, think again. Remember, this isn't
the *Sportscenter* or *Beavis and Butthead*–watching ex; this is the guy who
will proudly watch cooking shows and indie films. The more mature groom is not only interested in his wedding, he's opinionated.
After all, he's probably footing the bill this time (with you of
course) and he wants his imprint on the day. He wants certain food,
music, invitations, and why not? He's the groom!

If he's a first-time groom, watch out. He definitely wants things
his way. My husband was so involved that if it weren't for him, we
may not even have had a wedding. I remember the scene:

A beautiful white sandy beach in Aruba, hours after he proposed. "We can elope," I say.

Blank stare, followed by a look of horror.

And there it was. My fiancé wanted a wedding.

I always thought guys liked the idea of skipping all the formalities, family, and festivities that come with weddings, opting for saving money and doing something fun, like getting married on an
island or in Vegas. Nope—not my man. It's as if he'd been the little
girl who grew up dreaming of that walk down the aisle (minus the
princess gown, of course).

To my surprise, having a traditional wedding was important to
him, and not just a simple ceremony followed by a champagne
brunch. Bobby wanted an elegant black-tie, live-band, open-bar

affair complete with a sit-down dinner at a classy hotel. *He* had a vision, too. Who knew? So how could I deny him? I didn't want him to miss out or have any regrets on one of the most important days of his life. He never had a wedding and this was what he wanted. It was important to him to celebrate his wedding with his family and friends. I found it kind of cute that he cared so much.

We knew we wanted our close friends and family at our wedding. We knew we wanted great food, music, and pictures. We made the decisions together. We agreed to prioritize the photography because the pictures are what last after the wedding. We wanted amazing pictures that would take us back to our special day every time we looked at them. We had no intention of scrimping on what would hold the key to our memories. Bobby helped me select our photographer and went with me to every appointment. And when it came time to register, he didn't just shuffle his feet behind me nodding to anything I held in front of him in an effort to speed the process along. He had opinions. We even got in a tiff in the linens section of a department store because we couldn't agree on a color for bath towels.

My dashing groom also:

- Went with my mom to meet with the hotel event manager when I was on deadline (I believed the two of them picked the cake).
- Went with me to meet band agents, see bands perform live, and then corresponded with the bands via fax and phone.
- Created the surprise letters that asked our attendants to stand up for us in our wedding.
- Called all over to find restaurants for the rehearsal dinner and inquired about space, menus, and prices.
- Stayed late at work making our rehearsal dinner invitations on his computer.
- Went with me to three separate appointments to select an artistic ketubah (Jewish marriage contract).

- Went with me to register at several places.
- Wrote his own vows.
- Wrote his own speech.

He was unbelievable. Completely involved. Merely showing that he cared wasn't his plan. He had a say in the day—our day. I loved that our wedding was a priority to him and he wanted to get involved. I didn't have to pester him or bribe him—he just wanted to be there. And sure enough, it was a predictor of how he'd be with other big life moments. (Fast forward a couple of years—he went to all of my doctor appointments with me when I was pregnant.)

My groom had the right idea. I'm so happy we didn't elope. I love looking at our wedding pictures, where we are surrounded by our family and friends. I'm glad we shared our wedding with our loved ones.

What's a Groom to Do?

The traditional bridal magazines print "to do" checklists for the guys, similar to those for the gals. According to one publication, for example, 6 to 12 months before the wedding the groom should choose his attendants, select his attire, brainstorm ideas for the groom's cake, and choose boutonnieres for his groomsmen. Call me crazy, but I get the feeling a groom isn't concerned about these things—let alone 12 months before the wedding. Is your engagement even that long?

So what is your groom to do? Well, it depends on his interest level and available time. But there are probably plenty of things he'd enjoy doing. Maybe creating the multi-candle table centerpieces would interest him. Perhaps he has a cool way to display the place cards. You can ask if he wants to design a creative seating arrangement. He may bring a fresh perspective to the typical wedding design and set-up practices. Don't shoo him away if he wants to move in on what's long been considered bridal territory. Heck, if he wants to pick linens, let him. Better yet, welcome him.

The only time I veer from this recommendation is if the groom starts making decisions that aren't necessarily for the good of the wedding. For example, if he gets carried away and starts offering outlandish decorating ideas that don't match your budget *or* your taste, you may need to have a little talk with him to mellow him out. He may need a breather and not even know it. After all, he's probably new to the hands-on planning.

Some grooms need a little nudge to get motivated. You'll want to watch out for the helpless act. I promise you, if he is in good health, he can dial a phone number. Maybe he does everything in his power not to pick up the phone at home because he claims "it's always for you," but you need to let him start dialing now, before he expects this to be your job always. He also can research pricing and availability. He can find the band, book the hotel rooms, figure out your transportation options, take his kids shopping for outfits, buy his own attire, hire the band, track down special songs, create a map for out-of-town guests, confirm details with vendors, and— my favorite—write thank-you notes. There are endless things he can do. You want him to get involved.

Keys to a Happy Engagement

• *Let him have his dream.* If you've been married before and you want to stay away from the big frou-frou wedding, that's understandable, but if it's your groom's first wedding and he wants a big blowout, you need to respect his wishes. It's not that bad to dress up, look gorgeous, have everyone make a fuss over you, and dance the night away with the love of your life.

• *Pick your battles.* You've probably heard this relationship advice a million times but it's crucial during the wedding planning process—a time when true colors really come out. One bride I interviewed wanted her invitations to read "black tie optional," but her fiancé felt so strongly about having them read "black tie" that she let him have his way. It wasn't a huge issue for her, and she liked that he felt good about the decisions he made.

• *Don't ignore your groom.* People get swept up in the mind-set that it's the bride's day. Sometimes your fellow may not know how involved he should get, because everyone is making a constant fuss over you. Help him feel special too. The best thing of all is to remind him every day how much you love him.

Wedding Day Reflections

My husband took care of the majority of the reception planning. He selected the site, menu, DJ, honeymoon, and his attire. He had been to many weddings and conventions and knew what he did and didn't like.

—Beth

When you get stressed out about juggling the planning with your career, the kids, or both, just take a step back and think about why you are doing this. You are not in this alone. Your fiancé probably wants to help. If you don't have time to coordinate your schedules to conquer every appointment together, sit down and divvy up the duties. You know how important partnership is. Your wedding is a great time to start making decisions together, if you haven't already.

If your honey feels strongly about renting classic cars to cruise through town after the ceremony, then let him have his wish. While you're at it, let him take care of the details. Getting your groom involved in the planning process means one more set of

Alexandra's Dream Come True

I always dreamed of having a wedding under the big maple trees in front of my grandmother's house. It was where my mother and aunt were each married, and I wanted to continue the tradition. My first husband was adamantly opposed to anything but a simple ceremony, so we got married in a hotel rooftop garden with a judge officiating and only family in attendance. Then we walked to another hotel for dinner. It was pleasant but nothing to write home about. I was 28. For my second wedding my husband, Michael, was much more accommodating. I was 33 and he was 38 and taken with the romance of continuing the family tradition. He loved my 92-year-old grandmother and was thrilled that she was letting us use her home. We paid for our wedding and had a guest list of almost 200 people.

My husband was part of the process from the start. We took out an equity line of credit on his house at his suggestion. He's a chef, so he made all the food decisions. He kept me sane during a very stressful half-year period prior to the wedding, when there was a lot of upheaval in my family. I also think he was always cognizant of the terrible experience I had the first time I tried to have the wedding of my dreams. He made sure our wedding was exactly the way I wanted it.

hands helping to make phone calls and manage the fine details of planning an event around a dozen different vendors.

When It's Not His First Time

Here second-time grooms share their wedding thoughts.

At 21, I was way too young to get married. My first wedding was very traditional with around 50 people in a church. I didn't get involved in the planning. I didn't have the maturity to know what to ask or to think things through. At my second wedding I was involved in everything, from picking the ceremony and reception sites to selecting the music. The priest who performed our ceremony was wonderful, but the greatest part was seeing my bride standing in the front of the church in her wedding dress.

—JIM

I was 30 at my first wedding and 33 at my second, which I helped plan with my bride in eight months. We got married at a renovated old mill house. The wedding was semiformal with about 80 people, and our ceremony was outside in the gardens. We paid for our wedding ourselves, so money was a concern, but we also had a lot of people coming in from out of town, so we wanted a location that would be easy for our guests to get to. The highlight was seeing Katy's face filled with happiness.

—CHRIS

There were 150 people at my first wedding. I was 25 and it was on a golf course at a country club. For my second wedding, my wife and I had 28 guests at a hotel. We both had been married before and we wanted something small with just family and close friends. We split the costs, and the entire experience was enjoyable and more subtle than my first wedding. There was no pressure. At my first wedding everything was timed to the minute. We had a schedule dictating when the cocktail hour was, when the toast was, when we had to cut the cake, and so on. I felt like I could only enjoy the party in little increments of time, and then we were interrupted for another thing on the schedule.

—MIKE

My first wedding was at a university chapel when I was 24. It was informal with about 90 people. My second wedding was a nonreligious, elegant affair for 120 people.

We went to see most of the vendors together. I really cared about the service, costs, and the food. We also created a list of who would take care of certain duties. Watching old friends mix with new friends and family and having the people we love celebrating with us in the same place was the best. It was also great knowing that we paid for and pulled off our amazing day.

—JON

I was 23 at my first wedding and there were 150 people. I was 31 at my second wedding and it was bigger—225 people. My engagement was pretty stress-free. I realized early on that the wedding was my mother-in-law's party (I married a first-time bride). The highlight of my wedding was seeing my bride walk down the aisle. It was the most beautiful sight I had ever seen. I also liked giving my speech. It gave me the opportunity to tell everyone I loved and cared about just what my wife meant to me. As a second-time groom, I felt excitement with small amounts of caution. I knew getting married to my wife was the right decision, but I was also aware that she knew I had experienced some of the "wedding stuff" before. I wanted to take it all in and make sure my wife fully understood that this wedding was going to be everything for both of us.

—BOB

Let's Hear It for the Groom

Here, two first-time grooms share their thoughts about marrying second-time brides. (Yes, Bobby is my husband, not to be confused with second-time groom Bob, above.)

I proposed on a beach in Aruba and the planning started immediately. (Due to the high cost of overseas phone calls, guys should think twice about where they propose.) My wife originally suggested a small wedding or even eloping, but that was out of the question. Because we agreed to a somewhat short engagement, many things had to be done rather quickly. Top priorities on my list were location, a great photographer, great food, and a nice rehearsal dinner.

I registered with my bride, viewed the possible locations, met with the bands and photographer, and planned the rehearsal dinner. Despite the exhausting travel, numerous calls, and hundreds of worries, I knew it was all worthwhile when I saw my bride under the chuppah before the ceremony. Whether it was my bride's second, third, or fourth wedding, it was my first wedding and our first wedding, and I wanted it treated that way!

—BOBBY

I'm 31 and I recently got married for the first time to a second-time bride. I was very involved with planning our out-of-town wedding. It was my idea. We had a lot of out-of-towners so we decided to have a wedding in Florida, even though we are from the Midwest. This way, everyone could travel to a fun place. I secured the date and the location: Hard Rock Hotel in Orlando. It was such a cool place, with music going all the time, I figured our guests had to have a good time. We had 65 people and I wanted to have a lot of say, partly because we were paying for most of the wedding. I checked out the florist and the band—we wanted upbeat music instead of the old traditional stuffy music.

Planning a wedding out of state is sometimes inconvenient, but my advice is not to paralyze yourself with the small stuff and remember to enjoy your wedding. I've seen people let something ridiculous like a napkin stop them from having a good time. Think about the things that are going to be important to you on the big day.

—STEVE

Grooms Get Their Say

For all you gals who lament to your friends, "I wish I knew what he was thinking," here's a treat for you. I've got the real scoop from grooms about what they were thinking pre-wedding:

Grooms are thinking they don't want to wear an uncomfortable tuxedo or shoes and they don't want to write thank-you notes. They just want to get married.

—MIKE

I was wondering if everything being planned was just too much, but it turned out to be wonderful.

—JON

I'd find myself asking, "How can I afford this, where can I cut costs," which later turned into, "Oh who cares, let's just do it."

—BOBBY

I was thinking about costs. We paid for the wedding ourselves since we were both in our 40s and it was a second marriage for both of us. I didn't want to be "cheap," I just wanted to figure out where to spend the money. For example, should I have better wine at the reception and spend less on flowers? Do I do a less-fancy invitation and go for an extra night at the Ritz?

—JIM

All guys are going to be a bit freaked out about the finality of marriage, especially on the big day. That doesn't mean they don't love you or that they are having second thoughts. It just means they are normal.

—STEVE

I was thinking I just wanted my fiancé to be happy. But I was also thinking I'd love to have a party for one-tenth of the cost and bank the rest.

—BOB

Let him off the hook when it comes to little details like monogrammed napkin font choices. Remember that it's a lot hotter to wear a tuxedo outside in

*the summer than a sleeveless dress, and understand that some men just
don't dance.*

—CHRIS

What No One Tells the Groom

*Not enough men think about what sort of wedding they want. If they wait
too long to get in on the planning, they'll get steamrolled out of the process.*

—JIM

There will be family squabbles because everyone has an opinion.

—BOBBY

His boutonniere is way too big.

—CHRIS

So Happy Together

Now that you are working together, be sure to take time out during your engagement to play and truly enjoy one another. (Yes, you can let go of your binder and kick back with your man.) After all, that's why you're calling rental companies and interviewing bands to begin with—because you're in love with an amazing guy and you want to celebrate your relationship and your commitment to one another with a wonderful wedding.

Fine Dining

THE CATERING, CAKES, AND CONTRACTS

At a recent catering conference, a famous wedding designer told the audience that the most important element of the wedding is the food; it's where the planning of your concept or ambiance begins. You may not agree with him, but the fact remains that a large portion of your wedding budget will probably go toward food and drinks. You want to choose wisely, because these two items can make your guests very happy (or not). Fortunately, there is more variety in wedding fare today, from appetizers to desserts.

Will It Be Brunch, Buffet, or a Seated Dinner?

When deciding on your dining style, you should think about the size of the room, available kitchen space, your budget, and the level of hospitality you want to create, says Shelley J. Pedersen, past president of the National Association of Catering Executives and owner of Beyond Cuisine, Inc., a boutique-style catering company in Atlanta (www.beyondcuisine.com).

You'll also want to factor in your personality. If you and your fiancé can't stand to dance, you may like the more low-key feel of a daytime wedding, such as a brunch or an afternoon tea. A brunch can be scrumptious with fresh pastries, waffles, crepes, and omelets, while a tea can be elegant with delicious scones presented on footed plates and gorgeous china. (You'll also be spared a hefty bar bill with either of these options.)

However, if you and your honey plan on dancing until the wee hours of the morning, you'll probably want a dinner reception. You have several choices of evening dining styles—and as long as you pick food you love, you can't go wrong.

Dining styles also may be influenced by what's popular where you live. In the Midwest, seated dinners are favored, but in the South, buffets and hors d'oeuvres receptions are common.

All Hors d'Oeuvres, All the Time

A cocktail reception offers guests an array of hors d'oeuvres, and you don't have to bring the mingling to a halt in order to move guests into the main dining room for dinner. You get an array of food (roughly 6 to 10 choices) from bruschetta to baby lamb chops. You can save money on food (there is less of it), and because there aren't as many tables, you can save money on centerpieces, linens, and tableware. But while your friends and family are eating less, they are drinking more at the cocktail reception, so the bar bill may be steep. Overall, the all-hors-d'oeuvres reception can be elegant and fun.

The Line Forms Here

A buffet can be large and lavish, but that line thing is never a crowd pleaser. If you have two buffets set up, you can eliminate the everlasting line. A buffet isn't necessarily a money-saver, as many believe. The caterer actually has to prepare more food than needed for a sit-down dinner because guests can frequent the buffet as many times as they like.

Around the World

Food stations are usually the most creative, and they can reflect your love of exotic foods. You can have an around-the-world-type evening with Asian noodle dishes at one station and Spanish tapas at another. Some setups even let you make your own food, or at least slather on your own choice of sauces. Another bonus: There is less labor. Several food and beverage stations can be a good alternative to a crowded buffet.

Second-Time Smarts

To find a caterer in your area, contact the National Association of Catering Executives at www .nace.net, or call 410-997-9055.

Please Be Seated

The seated dinner is very popular for second weddings. Some couples want their guests to relax and be served. A sit-down dinner is usually formal, and everyone eats together at the same time. This is an elegant way to go, and your guests will appreciate the beautiful presentation of each course that's brought to them.

Choosing Your Caterer

Services and prices vary from caterer to caterer. Some offer food, period. Others provide food, drinks, the wait staff, linens, tables and chairs, and more. The caterer at your first wedding may have handled only the food, but today many caterers are also wedding coordinators. They will line up the music, florist, photographer,

Book Ahead

Different caterers book up at different rates, but some times are busier than others. "Thanksgiving, Christmas, New Year's, and Valentine's Day are in 'engagement season'—that's when we get all the calls," says Valerie Vollmer, director of catering for The Plug Nickel Restaurant & Catering in Westlake Village, California. Vollmer adds that her second-time brides spend 25 percent more on food than do first-time brides.

and officiant, and they'll even run the rehearsal. Of course, you pay for the extended service. Make sure you and your caterer have an understanding of how involved you want him or her to be.

If your reception site has an in-house caterer, then your search is over because you probably can't bring in an off-site caterer. But even if you aren't shopping around for a caterer, you'll still want to ask your caterer questions (see "Questions to Ask Your Caterer" later in this chapter).

Ask to see the caterer's portfolio and schedule a tasting so you can try the foods you'd be serving at your wedding. In addition to having a great reputation for fabulous food and presentation, the caterer should understand what you are looking for and be open to your menu suggestions. You want to make sure you feel comfortable talking to your caterer. If you don't like his or her personality, it could be hard for you to deal with that person now and throughout your wedding. Our hotel caterer let us add appetizers and desserts not found on the standard event menus. Hire a caterer who will work with you. If you must have a certain dessert and you are offered only two choices, that caterer simply won't do.

Creating Your Menu

Perhaps now that you're older, your tastes are more sophisticated and you prefer sushi over pigs in a blanket. You won't find cheese cubes and chicken wings at elegant second weddings. They may have been popular at the wedding parties you attended right out of college, but at second weddings, you see food and wine that reflect more mature taste buds. I've talked to couples who prioritized the food at their weddings, putting plenty of thought into the menu rather than just circling "option A" on the caterer's menu sheet. There are also couples who did something different with their wedding menu and offered cuisine such as Caribbean, Latin, French, or Southwestern.

I constantly hear that the best part about wedding food is the hors d'oeuvres. Few guests rave about the chicken breast, but they're probably wishing they could grab a few more coconut shrimp skewers or miniature crab cakes. In second weddings, couples are willing to include unique hors d'oeuvres, such as alligator, sushi, pot stickers, and exotic vegetables, says Bill Hansen, founder and CEO of Leading Caterers of America, president of Bill Hansen's Culinary Events in Miami, and an instructor at the School of Hospitality Management at Florida International University.

Midnight Snacks

Some couples like to offer late-night snacks, like Krispy Kreme doughnuts (www.krispy kreme.com, or call 800-334-1243).

As a second-timer you know it's important for the food not only to look great, but to taste great. When you are deciding on your menu, think about the foods you and your fiancé like. What would make you happy? If you have special favorites, by all means make them part of your day. Just because you've been to 100 weddings in the past that served chicken doesn't mean you can't mix up the menu a bit. Perhaps you want your favorite comfort foods, so only risotto or pasta will do.

Another good approach is to bring out a recipe that's unique to the location of your wedding. Treat your guests to Cajun delights in Louisiana or deep-dish pizza in Chicago. You can also include some hometown favorites. If your fiancé is from the South, how about black-eyed-pea fritters or shrimp and grit cakes? Our hotel agreed to add a Michigan favorite to our dessert menu—Sanders Hot Fudge cream puffs. Sanders Hot Fudge is from Michigan. The fudge is served over a cream puff with vanilla ice cream inside. They were a big hit both with local guests and out-of-towners.

Anything goes for food in second weddings, but let the time of day and year be a guide. A plate of prime rib in the middle of August is too heavy; your guests will probably want something a little lighter, such as salmon.

If you've hired a professional and you've seen and tasted their creations but are still ambivalent about what food to select, ask the caterer what they would serve if it was *their* event.

And to help give you some ideas, I've included some sample menus in this chapter, plus the menu from my second wedding. I want to show you examples from some of the best in the business. I've included menus both from an on-site catering facility and an off-site catering company.

The world-class Four Seasons Hotel Atlanta (the only Five Star, Five Diamond hotel in Georgia) shares some of its menu choices:

Samples of Hors d'Oeuvres Available for Cocktail Receptions

Ahi Tuna Tartare on Wasabi Crisp

Lobster and Sweet Corn Salad on Toasted Corn Bread

Carmelized Vidalia Onion Tart with Goat Cheese

Teriyaki Marinated Beef Sate

New Zealand Lamb Chops with Mint Aioli

You can also have food stations set up during your cocktail hour:

Sushi Bar

Assorted Selection of Sashimi and Sushi*

- *Tuna Roll*
- *California Roll*
- *Salmon*
- *Yellow Tail*

*Prepared to order in the room by a Japanese Sushi Chef

Raw Bar

Assorted Oysters on the Half Shell

Jumbo Gulf Shrimp

Alaskan Snow Crab Claws

King Crab Legs

Florida Stone Crab Claws (seasonal—March to December)

Pasta/Risotto Station

Potato Gnocchi Pomodoro

Smoked Chicken and Mascarpone Ravioli with Basil Cream

*Wild Mushrooms, Rock Shrimp, and Asparagus Risotto
    Finished with Butter*

*Reggiano Parmesan Cheese and Herbs Served with House
    Baked Garlic Focaccia and Italian Rustic Breads*

Fajita Station

Grilled Chicken and Skirt Steak with Peppers and Onions

Soft Corn and Flour Tortillas

Pico de Gallo

Tomatillo Salsa

Guacamole and Queso Fresco

Caesar Salad Station

Hand Cut Romaine

Croutons

Shaved Cheese

Grilled Shrimp and Chicken

If stations aren't for you, here is a Four Seasons Hotel Atlanta
sample dinner menu:

Appetizer

Ratatouille Risotto with Parmesan Crisp

Soup

Old-Fashioned Cream of Chicken Soup with Dumplings

Salad

Organic Field Greens with Basil Marinated Tomatoes

Warm Goat Cheese Crouton

Tarragon Vinaigrette

Entrée

Hot Smoked Salmon Glazed with Sourwood Honey and
   Violette Mustard

Braised Cabbage and Caramelized Onions

French Lentils

Dessert

Duo of White and Dark Chocolate Mousse

Brandied Cherries

Chocolate Biscotti

Sample Menus

The creative and fun menu following is provided by Marley
Majcher, chief creative officer of The Party Goddess, a catering and
event planning company in Pasadena, California. Pricing is determined by the number and type of items selected from each menu.

ASIAN INFUSION

Passed Hors d'Oeuvres

Sushi Rolls with a Wasabi Ginger Sauce

California Rolls

Ginger Shrimp—Stuffed Mushrooms

Veggie Spring Rolls

Entrée Options

Smoked Chicken with a Cranberry Vinaigrette

Bay Scallops with Spinach, Pine Nuts, and a Sweet and
   Sour Dressing

Thai Noodles

Vegetable Fried Rice

Marinated Mushrooms

Salmon Dumplings with a Cucumber Relish

Pork Scallopini with Black-Eyed Pea Vinaigrette

Roast Chicken with a Wild Mushroom Stir-Fry

Dessert

Pineapple Coconut Sorbet

White Chocolate Macadamia Nut Cookies Dipped in Chocolate

Fresh Bananas Rolled in Coconut

Ginger Créme Brûlée

Biscotti

Refreshments

Hot or Cold Sake

Asian Beer

Specialty Martini and Cocktail Bars

Green Tea

JULIE AND BOBBY'S MENU

Our wedding was at a charming historic hotel, on a gorgeous
fall evening, but more important (at least for this chapter), the

food was amazing! How good? I actually sat down and ate at my own wedding. What a concept. Never mind the fact that I still had tables of friends to meet and greet, I was determined to enjoy my wedding dinner. We even have pictures of me chewing. (At my first wedding I don't think I had a morsel of food.) We were able to pick our favorites and we had a tasting. The tasting is crucial because you may find you'd like the chef to alter the way he or she prepares something. For example, we asked that at our wedding, the vegetables not be drenched in butter.

If you're curious about our food choices, check out our menu following.

Cocktail Reception (Hors d'Oeuvres Passed Butler Style)

Miniature Beef Brochettes

Spinach and Feta Cheese in Phyllo Pastries

Chinese Eggrolls

Goat Cheese with Sun-Dried Tomatoes and Basil on Toasted Baguettes

Shrimp Tempura

Dinner

Assorted Rolls (multi-grain, sourdough, whole wheat thyme, and cherry walnut) with Butter and Margarine

Three Cheese Ravioli with Garlic Cream Sauce

Caesar Salad

Chicken Piccata

Chef's Fall Mixed Vegetables

Plain Polenta Grilled

Dark and White Chocolate Mousse Torte

We also had a special dessert area after dinner and during dancing:

Two Coffee Stations

Freshly Brewed Coffee

Brewed Decaffeinated Coffee

Chocolate Shavings

Sugar Cubes

Cinnamon Sticks

Chantilly Cream

Sanders Sundae Bar

Fudge Brownies

Cream Puffs

Vanilla Frozen Yogurt

Sanders Hot Fudge

Fresh Whipped Cream

Chopped Nuts

Jimmies and Maraschino Cherries

A Sweet Table

Jumbo Chocolate Chip Cookies

Jumbo Oatmeal Cookies

Chocolate-Covered Strawberries

Chocolate-Covered Apricots

Big Bowls of Fresh Fruit

When you are explaining to your catering manager the type of food and atmosphere you want, don't be afraid to speak up. They get only one shot to get it right, so you might as well be very clear up front. At our wedding, we had specific instructions that the hotel distributed in writing to the maitre d', chef, and catering staff:

- *All* linen must be pressed and very crisp. Especially skirting.
- *All* china, glassware, and silverware must be cleaned and polished.
- Please have two *elegant* coffee stations with items displayed on silver trays. *Do not* use mugs. Must use coffee cups and saucers.
- Please prepare vegetables in light oil with no butter.
- Food must be flavorful and cooked appropriately.
- Presentation of food items should be perfect.

Wedding Day Reflections

We wanted a premium bar, excellent food, and plenty of it. We love appetizers, so we had six different kinds: crab cakes, duck, spring rolls, tenderloin, stuffed mushrooms, and coconut shrimp. For dinner we chose a dual entrée of grilled salmon and chicken with mushrooms. The dessert table was an assortment of amazing cakes, pies, and mousses. We also had a cappuccino/coffee/espresso bar that our guests thought was awesome!

—Jessica

Quick Catering Tips

- Try not to repeat ingredients. You don't want corn in your soup, corn in your salsa, and then corn muffins.

- It's a myth that a buffet is less expensive than a sit-down dinner. It all depends on the food. Sometimes it's more expensive to offer enough of a variety with a buffet than to serve three courses. Plus, with a buffet, guests can fill up their plates as often as they want, so you may need to have more food.

• Some couples save money by offering one entrée instead of offering a choice.

• Offer colorful ingredients so the dish looks more savory. White mashed potatoes blending in with a white plate probably won't look very exciting.

Wedding Day Reflections

I was responsible for paying the caterer and I did so in haste, after the cocktail hour. I wound up tipping her close to 75 percent of the entire bill. She said nothing and kept the money, and then didn't return our phone calls when we returned from our honeymoon. If I could do it differently, I would have waited to pay her until I was thinking more clearly.

—Jon

• If you want to offer a surf-and-turf-type of dinner, but your budget allows for only turf, you can compromise. How about a lower-priced fish or chicken main course with lobster and shrimp hors d'oeuvres?

• Throw in at least one fun surprise. Perhaps you'll offer hot cocoa for everyone at the end of the night. Other big late-night hits include burgers, hot dogs, pizza, caramel corn, tacos, and submarine sandwiches.

• Order some vegetarian plates for your guests who don't eat meat.

• If your caterer is providing serving pieces, china, and linens, make sure you see them first. You'll also want to have the caterer instruct his or her staff to make sure the linens are pressed and the serving pieces are polished and sparkling. The last thing you want is to spend good money on delicious appetizers and have the silver trays look like they were sitting in Grandma's attic for a year. You are hiring a professional who pays careful attention to detail, so such a request shouldn't result in any sighs or eye rolling.

• If you are having an outdoor, home, or tent wedding, make sure you set aside an area for the caterer to prep and set up the burners.

• Be sure to arrange for a special kids' menu. Let the caterer know well in advance that you have children and you'd like him or her to come up with some creative dishes for the kids.

Martinis or Champagne?

When you got married the first time, your family may have had one main decision to make regarding drinks: whether or not to have an open bar. The first wedding was out of your control, but now you can make the decisions. An open bar is the way to go. A cash bar is insulting. Who carries cash to a wedding anyway?

Things have changed when it comes to spirits. You have many more decisions to make. But fortunately they are fun decisions. For example, do you want a martini bar or frozen drinks? Presentation counts—do you want chic colored glasses to serve drinks in? Will

Think Drinks!

Worried the typical bar choices will seem a bit stale? Marley Majcher, of The Party Goddess, offers some creative drink ideas:

- Lemon drop martinis with colored-sugar rims
- Chocolate martinis with cocoa or coffee-dipped rims
- Floating raspberries or blueberries in champagne
- Tequila sunrises for a brunch
- Peach, banana, or strawberry margaritas
- Orange-grapefruit spritzers
- Creating your own names for drinks offered at the bar

the alcohol flow from an ice luge? Will you offer specialty drinks? Perhaps you'd like to have a wine tasting for your cocktail hour.

Your options are endless because: a) Your mom is not planning an old-school-type wedding, and b) you can let your creativity and personality show in every detail, from the flavored vodka to the swizzle sticks. Some couples are choosing to offer a large selection of wines by the glass and others want to serve a special mixed drink created just for them.

Second-Time Smarts

Inform the bar staff that you do not want beer cans or bottles offered at your wedding. Beer should be served in a glass.

• Liquor can be billed by the bottle or drink, or worked into the price of the meal. Make sure you're not being charged for alcohol for the children.

• Be sure to offer non-alcoholic drinks. (At my wedding we even had the hotel offer caffeine-free diet colas for the guests who can't drink caffeine.) It's also nice to offer some beverages that are not carbonated.

• In addition to paying for wine, you'll usually need to tack on a service charge if you want wine served at the table.

Fun Touches
• Decorating martini glasses with cake gels.
• Freezing fruit in ice cubes.
• Dipping the rims of glasses in colored sugar.

If you're stumped on how far your dollar will go, The Party Goddess shares her cheat sheet. Be sure to consider your guests and the time of year.

• Champagne: Five glasses to a bottle.
• Wine: Four glasses to a bottle.
• Ice: Half a pound per person.

- Cocktail napkins for hors d'oeuvres: Two per person.
- Beverage napkins: Two and a half per person.

Contract Checklist

❑ Your name and all contact information

❑ Name of caterer and business and caterer's contact information: phone, pager, cellular, and e-mail

❑ Date and time of wedding

❑ Exact location of the wedding and specifically where the cocktails and reception will take place

❑ What you are getting and the time of service from start to end

❑ The exact time frame the caterer will be at the wedding and names of other personnel who will be on duty

❑ Backup plan in writing if they should cancel, including whether or not they will line up a replacement

❑ Caterer's cancellation policy

❑ Minimum head count you are obligated to pay for

❑ All fees—including sales tax and gratuities

❑ The specific food and beverages being served

❑ The exact quantities of pricier foods like lobster

❑ Fee for vendors' meals (photographer, musicians)

❑ Attire for wait staff and bartenders

❑ Staff-to-guest ratio

❑ Due dates for deposit and payments

❑ Due dates for final menu selection and final head count

❑ Caterer's signature

Professionally Speaking

Cappuccino bars are always a hit. According to Bill Hansen of Bill Hansen's Culinary Events in Miami, "after-glow" stations are in demand. Most of his weddings now include a special station offering espresso, cappuccino, international coffees, cognacs, cordials, and liqueurs along with some bite-sized desserts.

Questions to Ask Your Caterer

- What is your specialty?
- Are you licensed in the state, and insured?
- What services do you offer? Do you provide a serving staff, bartenders, napkins, tablecloths, and other necessities?
- What are your favorite events to do?
- How many wedding receptions have you catered?
- Can you give us some references of events similar to the one we are planning?
- How large are your portions?
- Do you have sample menus and a price list?
- What equipment do you provide?
- Do you supply chairs, tables, linens, china, flatware, and stemware?
- What is your staff's attire?
- Is setup and cleanup included in the price?
- What are your fees?
- What items are taxed?
- What extras aren't covered in the package?
- Is the gratuity included for the bartenders and wait staff?
- Is there an overtime charge?
- Do we get a detailed proposal spelling out all charges?
- Does the quote include a choice of entrées, or would we have to pay to offer our guests a choice?
- When is the final payment due?
- What is your deposit and cancellation policy?

Cakes

Sometimes the cake is included in your reception package. That can save you a lot of money, because cakes can run hundreds or thousands of dollars. But if you want a cake that's particularly unique or exquisite, you'll need to call in the specialty cake makers.

You don't have to have a standard white wedding cake, but if you want to, go ahead. White cakes aren't reserved just for first-time brides. If you want to do something different for your second wedding, you can have cheesecake, torte, pie, or an array of several small cakes. You can have brownies or peanut brittle, for that matter. Lately, stacked cupcakes are showing up at weddings. Nowadays, pretty much anything can be dressed up in a cake-like fashion. Couples even have wedding cakes made out of doughnuts.

Let your cake express your relationship. For example, Janice chose to have a lighthouse top her wedding cake because her wedding was seaside and her husband proposed at a lighthouse.

Bake Me a Cake As Grand As You Can

Your possibilities for wedding cake are endless. Today's flavors include chocolate, carrot, peanut butter, praline, lemon, coconut, and hazelnut, covered in fondant, marzipan, buttercream, or royal icing. Cake designers can create cakes as colorful or as whimsical as you like. From chapels to castles, you name it, someone can probably bake it. The catch is that the mega-fabulous five-tiered cakes adorned with gum-paste flowers will cost a pretty penny.

As for the look, the cake designer or bakery should have pictures of cakes they've designed, which can give you some ideas. You can also bring in pictures of cakes you like. If you really want something different, you want a baker who will work with you on coming up with exactly what you are looking for.

Questions to Ask the Cake Maker

- What kinds of cakes do you make?

- What is your specialty?

- How do you price your cakes?

- Will you make different flavored fillings for each tier?

- Can you customize the cake to include the colors of our wedding?

- Do you deliver the cake to the reception site? What are your delivery costs?

- Do you have a backup plan in case anything happens to our cake? Would you supply another cake?

- May we sample the cake and fillings we are interested in?

- When do you need the deposit?

- When are final payments due?

- What is your cancellation policy?

If what you have in mind isn't in their portfolio, and they demand you pick from their book, then they're not the designer for you. However, if you are selecting a cake from an inclusive package, you will probably need to pick one of the baker's standard cake designs.

As I mentioned earlier, the cake was not a top priority for us. Ours was part of the hotel's package. We chose a yellow cake filled with fresh strawberries and whipped cream and covered with white frosting. Our florist decorated it beautifully with fresh flowers. Pretty basic. I've talked to brides who want just the opposite—they practically judge a wedding by the cake. Some bring in out-of-state cake designers for their wedding so they can have a designer who is written up in all the national magazines, or the baker who creates confections for celebrities. Often these look more like works of art, almost too pretty or too elaborate to eat, but they taste as good as they look.

Whatever kind of cake you choose, don't overlook the little details, like making sure the "cake table" is placed for prominent viewing. I was at a wedding where the wait staff set up the cake in the very back of the room, practically blocked by the musicians' equipment, and hardly anyone saw it.

If you have children, you can skip the groom's cake (a Southern tradition) and instead have special small cakes made for each child. A nice way to include your children in the reception is to give them a task they'll love: Let them bring the cake into the reception area and have them help you cut it. That way you can all eat the first few bites as a family, and you're sure to get some great pictures.

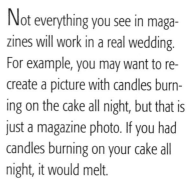

Professionally Speaking

Not everything you see in magazines will work in a real wedding. For example, you may want to re-create a picture with candles burning on the cake all night, but that is just a magazine photo. If you had candles burning on your cake all night, it would melt.

—Carol Marino, president and owner of A Perfect Wedding, Inc., in Washington, D.C.

Setting the Mood

BRINGING YOUR THEME TO LIFE

This chapter is all about the look, the mood, the feel, the ambiance. You enter the beautiful reception area and you are taken with the fresh scent of the flowers and the amber glow of the candles. You see the vibrant colors and feel the velvety textures. You hear the music and laughter and know you are in for a good time. Love is in the room, and it looks beautiful.

When creating your scene, think of the mood you want to evoke. Remember Beth and Scott's cabaret-style setup with food stations in chapter 4? "We wanted to cut out a lot of the stuff we'd seen a zillion times at weddings when we were younger," says Beth.

What kind of atmosphere really represents you and your husband-to-be? Are you music lovers? Into the outdoors? Are you sports fanatics or die-hard movie fans? Think about what you want to incorporate into the day. Some golf lovers choose to get married at a golf course and let the theme spin from there with golf-related invitations, favors, and hotel guest bags. Movie lovers may want late-night treats of popcorn, Raisinettes, and licorice. Did someone let you borrow their downtown loft? You can rent some cool couches, serve martinis, and play funky music while you glide down the curvy staircase in your sexy sheath dress.

The word *theme* doesn't have to suggest thoughts of a six-year-old's Disney-motif birthday party. A theme doesn't have to be juvenile. It can be sophisticated and elegant. You are looking for a style, the common link that will pull everything together. For example, you can base a theme simply around color. If you like blue and purple, you can have blue and lilac flowers on the cake, and the colors can appear on your invitations, your bridesmaids' bouquets, your thank-you notes, even your groom's attire (he can wear a purple tie). If you're having a Southern wedding, consider featuring regional flowers such as camellias, dahlias, hydrangeas, gardenias, lilacs, or peonies.

Cheryl Mayfield Brown, a second wedding coordinator based in Charlotte, North Carolina (www.twiceisnicebride.com), decided to help other brides after her second wedding was a big hit. She took the princess concept to another level. Her fairy-tale theme started with the invitations. Guests received a storybook with a "once upon a time" tale of Cheryl's wish to find her prince. Cheryl wore a headpiece and carried a crystal ball with roses and greenery. She glued crystals to her $90 dress, and her husband wore a cape and hat. Guests received cups of rose petals to sprinkle on the floor. Trumpet players opened the ceremony, and the Friday afternoon affair—held at a mansion—was complete with a fairy godmother who walked down the aisle. "Many vendors couldn't see our vision, but luckily our caterer got it," says Cheryl. "She made our cake and put an old Fisher-Price toy castle on top of it." Cheryl had her dream wedding—elegant with a touch of whimsy.

What Is Elegance?

Elegance can be simple or extravagant. Elegance can be achieved on a budget or with an unlimited bank account. It's not about how much you spend; it's how you choose to spend it. You can have an elegant party for two. You can bring elegance to parties or locations not often considered elegant, such as a seaside inn or a rustic ranch. A weathered, wooden barn can be transformed. Some couples get married at ruins. Crumpled, chipped, and cracked columns left standing provide the perfect backdrop for winding vines or lush flowers and anything else your imagination dreams up. You can add beauty and grace to any affair with the help of lighting experts, special event coordinators, floral designers, and of course your own amazing ideas and experience.

Subtle details can tie into a theme. If you're going a little bit Western, how about an antique wagon in a corner or a cowboy hat hanging behind the bar? The theme doesn't have to be cheesy or gimmicky. If you are both movie buffs, an Oscar night theme is an interesting way to personalize your reception. You could get married in an old theater, post your names up on the marquee, set the stage as your dance floor, and serve popcorn fresh from a popcorn maker in elegant champagne flutes.

ANNE'S STORY

My first wedding was traditional—the tables were covered with eyelet tablecloths. I decided to go in a totally different direction for my second wedding: 300 people at a downtown Los Angeles warehouse. The cocktail room had white carpet down the center, a Lucite-and-metal bar with an art deco "angel" coming out from the wall, white spandex table covers, branches, vases of wheat grass, a wall of votive candles, and other metal containers hanging from the wall filled with grass and white flowers. The main reception room was divided into "his" and "her" sections. "His" side contained cream-colored linens, gold candelabras, white Casablanca lilies, white roses, ivy, and chandeliers. "Her" side had leopard tablecloths with orange high-pile fur overlays, trimmed in fuchsia marabou. The centerpieces were metal air conditioner and dryer parts stuffed with orange, magenta, and yellow roses, orchids, ranunculus, and wheat grass.

———————————

Themes in general are very popular, says Amy E. Goodman, an editor at *In Style Weddings* magazine. She says a favorite theme for celebrity second-timers is "There's no place like home." The homeward-bound brides and grooms include Julia Roberts, Mel Harris, Elizabeth Perkins, Pierce Brosnan, and Paul McCartney.

Don't dismiss the outdoor or at-home wedding as "cheap." You can transform tents into ballrooms with chandeliers, dance floors, and Chiavari chairs. Home weddings actually can be more expensive than hotel weddings because everything must be rented, from the tent and tables to the bathrooms and salt and pepper shakers, says Los Angeles wedding coordinator Mindy Weiss, who plans many celebrity weddings and is known for creating a cozy atmosphere with props such as sofas, chairs, and chandeliers. Mindy says 20 percent of her business is second weddings. She recently planned Brooke Shields' second wedding to Chris Henchy, and Charlie Sheen's second wedding to Denise Richards. Mindy shares some tips for achieving intimate elegance in wedding décor:

- Enhance an entrance with fabric to add romance.
- Rent charger plates for the tables.
- Keep linens neutral, in ivory or whites, and bring out color with flowers.

- Add trees to warm up a ballroom.
- Use a mix of rectangular tables for eight and traditional rounds.
- Put couches by the dance floor to create a living-room vignette instead of a ballroom look.

Searching for Inspiration

If you aren't sure what décor you want, look through magazines or books for ideas. Don't restrict yourself to wedding magazines; you may find an interesting idea in a decorating or gardening book. Visit different reception sites on weekends and sneak a peek at the décor. Your florist may have pictures of a wedding in his or her portfolio that you'd like to replicate with a little tweaking. Maybe your wedding gown will inspire you. You may want a Roaring 20s affair to follow

Far-Out Themes

Marley Majcher of The Party Goddess (www.thepartygoddess.com) in Pasadena, California, often orchestrates theme-based parties. Some of her specialties are Moroccan, Thai, Zen, Balinese, Polynesian/Island, and Garden of Eden. A couple of examples:

1. **Moroccan:** Brass candelabras, rose petals on the tables, mosaic vases for the flower arrangements, a belly dancer, Moroccan music, candles, big platters of Moroccan food served family style. Other accents include peacock feathers and gold tassels.

2. **Balinese:** Seats on the floor with pillows and low tables, bowls of water with floating flowers and candles, Balinese music, colorful Balinese umbrellas, henna tattoos.

your gown style. Be open to the possibilities. Think beyond the expected. You don't need to hit the bridal expos for ideas. How about home and garden shows or antiques shows? You might want to look at the iron gates or arches or find a unique table that would look fabulous at the entrance with place cards and flowers on top.

The theme can revolve around a place, season, era—whatever unifies your look. Here are a few ideas:

- **Bohemian:** Try colorful sari fabrics, candles, and beads.

- **Monochromatic:** If you want a crisp, modern look, you can keep the flowers, linens, and furnishings in the same color palette and mix different types of vases or arrangements. There are many different kinds of flowers you can use in the same color.

- **Holiday:** White lights. Red velvet table covers. Pinecones. You can get by with fewer decorations because many sites are often decorated for the holidays.

- **Winter:** Silver and white décor accented with white flowers, white tablecloths, birch trees, and silver vases, candlesticks, and serving pieces.

- **Autumn:** How about warm chocolate-brown-colored roses, or berries, hydrangeas, and roses in fiery colors? You can use minipumpkins to accent each guest's place setting.

- **Great Gatsby:** Think grand ballrooms, fountains, and art deco mirrors and chandeliers.

If you're having a small outdoor wedding at home, you can personalize your décor by mixing and matching heirloom antiques.

Combine special keepsakes from both of your families. The look will be one-of-a-kind, rich, and refined. If you happen to be an antiques lover and have been collecting treasures for years, your wedding is a great time to use them. Colorful china, from dessert plates to platters, can be combined with silver baskets and bud vases. Other beautiful pieces include antique punch bowls, vintage champagne buckets, and different styles of crystal glasses and goblets. I've heard of many unique accents for outdoor weddings. One of my friends displayed an antique bathtub to chill the bottled water.

If you're planning a reception mountainside or seaside, your wedding can be elegant and even formal. You have a blank canvas except for the sky, earth, and water. Any decorative elements you add will complement your breathtaking view. If you're having a wedding out West with horses rambling on the range, you don't have to resort to red-and-white checkered tablecloths. Deck the ranch-house reception with tables topped in terra-cotta-colored organza and lay Oriental rugs below. You can add lovely details to practically any site. Remember, crystal decanters, pearl-handled serving pieces, and silver candelabras will travel.

Another touch that's transportable is lighting—and it can do wonders. It's key for ambiance. Picture a house in the woods with lanterns hanging in the trees all around. You can also string lights above and around your seating area to give the illusion of a tent. For an indoor affair, stylish

Professionally Speaking

Whether you'd like simple or extravagant elegance, keep the focus on the tables. Avoid these décor mistakes:

• Having a beautiful book for guests to sign, but a plastic pen.

• Doing your own centerpieces. If you do, at least make them look like you went to some effort. Do the candles fit properly? Is there a large base so they will not tip over if you bump the table? Do the flowers fit in the vase?

—Valerie Vollmer, director of catering for The Plug Nickel Restaurant & Catering in Westlake Village, California celebrity wedding coordinators and lighting designers know the lighting secrets: amber or pink light bulbs or gels (colored transparent sheets placed over light fixtures to change light color) are the most flattering. If you can't change the bulbs, you can work with the lights you have by dimming them. Though lavender and pink are popular accent colors for tent ceiling lighting because they add softness, avoid these colors in the food display areas. You don't want the food to look pink!

If there is one common element that creates elegance, it's candles. Wedding coordinators, florists, and rental experts agree that there is nothing like candlelight. You'll often see their events sprinkled with tea lights, votive candles, or hurricane lamps. You can find candles in many colors, sizes, and scents on the Internet or at crafts stores. Candle Magic (www.candlemagic.net) based in Seacrest Beach, Florida, will custom-design candles for your wedding.

CAROLYN'S STORY

My first wedding was a week before Christmas (we gave away candy canes). It was traditional with a church choir and full mass. I was 29 and my parents paid for everything. I was 36 at my second wedding and it was also my husband's second wedding. We knew we wanted a simple and intimate wedding. We were mostly paying for it ourselves. We wanted to personalize our wedding as much as possible. We chose a garden theme, which was very symbolic of our love. We met when I hired my husband to design my backyard garden. We decided to get married in one of the beautiful gardens he designed, and then we had a reception at a restaurant about two blocks away for 70 people. The garden was already beautiful so we didn't need a lot of flowers, but we added a thick carpet of beautiful pink, white, and red rose petals. We designed our own invitations with dried flowers and wrote a poem about how we met. The invitations were presented as rolled-up scrolls in a gift box with dried flowers. Instead of numbering the tables, we named them after flowers and we offered a description of what each flower means. Our wedding programs had poems about flowers and were hand-made with floral paper. Each guest's plate had a pot of African violets (which means faithfulness) with a special hand-written message on the bottom of each pot, for them to take home as a gift. Our cake was done in a floral theme and it was topped with a big sunflower instead of a bride and groom. We felt relaxed by doing things less traditional, and our guests loved it. They still tell us they had never been to a wedding that special.

Having trouble drawing a line between tasteful and tacky? I asked experts from florists to caterers to share what *not* to include in your décor:

- Tulle
- Fake flowers or plants
- Lattice
- Runners
- Anything plastic
- A photo of the couple on an easel for guests to sign
- Poor-quality material

Professionally Speaking

My feeling is that chair covers look like you are trying to hide something that is ugly. Some chair covers rent for $20. I'd rather have a nice Chiavari chair.

—Michael Stern, president
of Regal Rents

What to Rent

If you opt for the at-home wedding, you'll need to call some rental companies and talk to different rental specialists. If your first wedding was at a hall, hotel, church, or temple, you may not be familiar with the party rental business. What's for rent today? "Anything," says Michael Stern, president of one of the biggest rental companies in the United States, Regal Rents (www.regalrents.com), based in El Segundo, California. "We've done some of the biggest and best celebrity weddings in Hollywood, and we do most of the big movie premieres." You can rent everything from bar stools with interchangeable cushions of your choice to fashionable sisal rugs when the grass beneath the tent just won't do. "Rentals are expensive, but you can bring in your own liquor with a tent wedding, and hotels charge outrageous amounts for liquor," he says. "It's the rentals versus the liquor."

Make sure your rental company handles after-hours calls, in case there are any problems. You can find a rental company in your area through the American Rental Association's consumer Web site: www.rentalHQ.com. For safety purposes, the association advises that you provide specific information about your site to your rental firm if you plan to rent a tent: Are there underground sprinklers, wires, cables, or sewer easements?

If you need a tent (or two), talk to your rental specialist about other items they offer. Many of the larger rental companies also offer event-planning services. They have staffers who can coordinate your vendors, and some even can provide vendors, from the florist to the caterer.

Things you can rent:

- Canopies
- Gazebos
- Portable bars
- Dance floors
- Linens
- Freestanding lights (i.e., Victorian-style street lamp)
- Tents
- China

- Stemware
- Flatware
- Heaters
- Air conditioners
- Portable restrooms
- Chandeliers
- Couches
- Chairs
- Rugs
- Screens
- Urns
- Wrought iron gates and architectural pieces

Inventory will vary depending on the size of the rental company. At Select Event Rentals (www.weparty.com), a large rental company based in Beltsville, Maryland, you can rent copper serving pieces, Christofle flatware, and Rosenthal china. At The Meetinghouse Companies, Inc. (www.Meetinghouse.com), an event company with a 32,000-square-foot warehouse filled with props, you can rent everything from trees to an antique buggy. Based in Elmhurst, Illinois, the firm has worked on themed weddings ranging from nautical and Renaissance to Halloween and Las Vegas. "Themes in second weddings reflect a personal memory spot that the couple may have, such as 'Caribbean' if they met on a cruise," says Deborah Borsum, owner and event planner.

Although I believe you can add elegance to any location, I don't really mean *you*. I mean your ideas executed through the help of trained professionals, such as lighting experts, florists, and rental company specialists. Unless you've had a great deal of practice, or your affair is very small, the do-it-yourself décor is hard to pull off. And even if you are a talented designer with wonderful taste, why would you want to bother with the stress of decorating your own wedding? You are entitled to your pre-wedding pampering like any

Rental Tips

Deborah Borsum of The Meetinghouse Companies shares her inside tips on what to know before booking a rental company:

• Make sure the company is enthusiastic, supportive, and interested in your upcoming event.

• Ask to see pictures of weddings they've handled.

• Ask for their most recent references, and call them.

• Find out how much experience the company has.

• Ask what systems they have in place to make sure orders are delivered accurately, on time, and in top-quality condition.

• Make sure you see the pieces you want to order before you order them. Don't rely on a photo. You want to look at the size, color, and condition of the items so you don't have to worry about something not being right on your wedding day.

• Find out if there are any additional fees such as union fees or permits.

other woman before her big day. You don't want to lose sleep the night before your wedding because you're worrying that you didn't drape enough fabric through the tent. Even if it costs more to enlist help, it's worth it. One of my friends stayed up late painting flowerpots the night before her wedding. I spoke with another bride who wanted to design her own centerpiece and became obsessed with creating a battery-operated display when she learned that her reception hall didn't allow candles.

You need the rental company experts to set up the tent and tell you where it should go. They will come to your site and evaluate the ground for a sturdy and flat area. With lighting, you don't want dear Dad climbing trees and stringing white lights throughout your backyard. Lighting professionals are trained to make the lighting look good in scale and from a distance.

Don't attempt to hang fabric throughout the tent's interior walls yourself. Remember, experts get professional training in how to take a vinyl or canvas tent wall and turn it into a luxurious room draped with chiffon.

If you're wondering where one finds a lighting specialist, event producer, special effects expert, tent supplier, or a vendor who can supply props like Greek columns or a fishing boat, you're in luck. There is an organization devoted to vendors in the special event industry. Mark Putnam, executive director of the International Special Events Society (ISES), says the society's Web site (www.ISES .com) can help you search for an event planner in your area. You can also search by specialty. "If you want further confirmation regarding the planner's ability, look for a certified special event planner (CSEP)," he says.

Linens

The linens (napkins and tablecloths) add texture and color and in some cases can completely energize tables and chairs. You can even layer fabrics, such as putting a sheer organza overlay on a solid, cotton tablecloth. You can select tablecloths by size, color, texture, and pattern. Think about your guest list, room size, and the colors that work best with the look you envision. Linens are available at several places. Your florist may offer them, or you can get them from your rental specialist, wedding coordinator, or the Internet.

Rental experts, wedding coordinators, and linen vendors are the first to tell you that even a plain, unattractive room can be transformed with the right linens. You want them to complement the color of the room without outshining the flowers.

If you are having a smaller wedding, and you want to do something different, how about using your own linens, such as vintage tablecloths for an afternoon outdoor tea or lush velour throws for a winter cocktail party?

Flower Power

For this chapter, I saved the best for last. Rental folks and photographers will stress the importance of nice chairs or chair covers, but I say there's nothing like a scene set with beautiful flowers. You don't need to spend a fortune or put flowers in every inch of the room. Floral arrangements don't have to be large to be striking. Some people may walk into a room and see table covers and chairs, but my eye goes immediately to the flowers. Perhaps it's in my blood as the granddaughter of a florist (my sweet Papa Jack created a visually stunning floral delight for my parents' wedding).

Visual presentation sets the mood for your reception and ceremony, and flowers have the most impact, creating beauty, color, and texture. Flowers are especially important to second-time brides. If your budget is limited, you are likely to select upscale flowers, even if it means having fewer or smaller arrangements. You want to be in sync with your florist, so make sure you meet two or three times before your wedding. Bring pictures of flowers, colors, and styles you like, as well as swatches of your gown's fabric and a photo of you in your gown (you can take a Polaroid picture at one of your fittings).

Second-time brides usually spend a larger portion of their budget on flowers. It's often a priority. Dale Morgan, co-owner of Blossoms in Birmingham, Michigan, says there are no flowers that are inappropriate for a second wedding. "I'm finding that second-time brides are looking for more glamorous flowers—something a little more understated-Hollywood-looking. They want to use richer colors."

CHRISTINE'S STORY

My first wedding was at a church and a five-star Victorian hotel. It was a princess wedding—we even had a white horse-drawn carriage take us from the church to the hotel. I went all out and probably spent about $40,000 of my parents' money. We had candelabras and flowers everywhere, limousines, and we served filet mignon. At my second wedding, I was 29, and I had more guests— about 130. It was my husband's first wedding and he wanted something outdoors. We were paying for most of the wedding ourselves, so our budget was a lot smaller than my first wedding budget. We decided on a Japanese garden, which was special to me because I'm

Grown in the U.S.A.

According to the California Cut Flower Commission:

• More than 65 percent of all domestically grown, commercially sold cut flowers are produced in California.

• Roses are the most popular fresh cut flower with consumers.

• California supplies approximately 125 million stems of all fresh cut roses sold to U.S. consumers. This accounts for 18 percent of all roses sold in the United States.

half Japanese. We had hors d'oeuvres, a dinner buffet, a dance floor, and a DJ. We added some unique cultural touches—my mom wore a ceremonial kimono, someone played Japanese guitar, and another man dressed up in gold Japanese garb and sang to us. We decorated with paper-bag luminaries with words like *love* and *longevity* written on them in Japanese. My first wedding was elaborate and I knew I couldn't "outdo" it, but I was so obsessed with having the perfect wedding. My second wedding allowed me to express myself in a deeper way. I had the courage to follow my heart. For example, I used red roses everywhere, and I didn't at my first wedding because I thought red was too dramatic. I wanted to create a wedding that reflected our style rather than focusing on what's "appropriate," which is what I was concerned about the first time around.

Jon S. Gerych, owner of Gerych's Distinctive Flowers and Gifts in Fenton, Michigan, has been doing wedding flowers for 35 years. He says 15 percent of his floral event company's business is second weddings. "Some brides have used us for their first and second weddings," he says. "Second-time brides may have a smaller wedding, but they have a bigger budget for flowers. They want nicer flowers and they are willing to spend more." He adds that the time of year doesn't matter because florists can get flowers from Australia, Holland, and Israel, if necessary.

Go ahead and have your florist put flowers where no flowers have been before. Don't just look down at the tables; look up. How about gorgeous ivy, roses, and other fresh flowers hanging from the chandeliers? Flowers look lovely adorning balconies and gates and framing doorways. Be creative with your table floral arrangements and accents. Sometimes the unexpected can add beauty and freshness. Mix fruit with flowers, or layer seasonal vegetables around the floral arrangement's base. Here are some good choices:

- Fruits: limes, lemons, oranges, berries, grapes,
  pears, plums, apples.
- Vegetables: avocados, artichokes, squash.
- Bear grass.
- Rocks, pebbles, twigs, moss.
- Herbs: rosemary, sage.
- Autumn leaves.
- Willow branches.

Florists rave that the color combo of hot pink and orange is a recent trend and that you can't go wrong with burgundy and burnt yellow for fall. But try not to base your decisions on trends. Choose what you love and what you think you are going to love years from now when you look at your wedding pictures. Remember, trends come and trends go.

What's your palette? Picking a color palette is a joy for second-time brides. Some brides told me they didn't have the guts to pick bold colors for their first wedding. Second-time brides aren't afraid to show their style. Light pink suits the blushing bride, but hot pink is passionate.

Here are some suggestions for color themes:

Red: Regal. Dramatic. You can't go wrong with the color of love. You've seen the red theme featured in magazines for several celebrity weddings. Possible reds: ranunculus, rose, dahlia, peony, tulip, mini calla lily.

Green: Earthy. Soothing. Whether you stick with shades of celery or lime, or mix in some white flowers, you can't go wrong with such a classic. Possible greens: hydrangea, calla lily, rose, chrysanthemum, viburnum, tulip, zinnia.

Blue and purple: Cool, striking colors. Rich jewel tones. You have many options: delphinium, hyacinth, violet, hydrangea, orchid, cornflower, stock, lilac, iris, freesia, rose, lisianthus, tulip.

Easy Elegance

Sayles Livingston, owner of Sayles Livingston Flowers in Adamsville, Rhode Island, has a non-traditional style. She uses lots of flowers for a lush look and she also uses off-the-wall items such as berries, vines, fruits, feathers, and rocks. These are some of her guidelines for elegance:

Elegant

- Romantic flowers
- Tall arrangements in silver calla vases
- Flowers tucked into napkins
- Floating gardenias in decorative bowls in the bathrooms
- Topiaries
- Nice fabric on tent poles

Not Elegant

- Cluttered tables
- Carnations
- Wedding favors
- Silly table names

The ballroom in the hotel my husband and I chose was beautiful, so we didn't have to dress up the room or hide the walls. There were gorgeous chandeliers and high ceilings.

Our linens were celadon green, and the floral centerpieces were in tall clear vases so they wouldn't obstruct peoples' view. We chose jewel tones for our flower colors—rich purples, magentas, reds, and blues mixed with greens. We had an array of flowers, including green hydrangeas and purple and red roses.

The area around the vases was layered with green leaves surrounded by votive candles. The arrangements weren't neat and tight. They were high with flowers sprouting out in various directions. Some flowers even drooped down. The centerpieces looked really different, colorful, and beautiful. I didn't use chair covers. The chairs had a burgundy fabric. Nothing special, yet nothing awful, and I simply didn't have the budget to bring in a slew of chairs for the night.

The décor for the chuppah usually falls under the florist's duties. Some florists get really creative because the chuppah is such a major focal point. You may decide on a covering built of branches and braided with flowers, or one constructed of columns and sheer fabric. I interviewed one bride whose floral designer imported a metal arch from Poland to serve as the chuppah. Ask to look through your florist's sample book for ideas.

Flowers that add elegance:

- Orchids
- Gardenias
- Roses
- Hydrangeas
- Lilies
- Freesia
- Ranunculus

MICHELE'S STORY

My second wedding reception was in my in-law's beautiful spacious and contemporary home. It was indoors and outdoors. We had tables with alternating cranberry-red and tangerine-orange silk tablecloths and flowers in oranges and purples. The pool was surrounded by votive candles that led guests to a tent draped with gorgeous fabrics. There were beautiful floral arrangements, gel uplights, and food stations set up along most of the tent walls. We had a separate tent for the vodka bar, and the band and the dance floor were in the middle with high- and low-top cabaret tables with silk tablecloths. Chandeliers were dimly lit in the tent, and candles added to the ambient lighting. The mood was absolutely elegant.

Second-Time Smarts

You don't need to break your budget ordering flowers for all the people who may walk down the aisle with you, as you did for your first wedding. In a second wedding you can shorten your list of bouquets and boutonnieres for you, your groom, and your children. Of course, if your close friends or your parents will participate in the ceremony, you may also want to include them.

Décor Tips

- You don't want to design your own flowers. Are you really going to spend the day creating arrangements for the entire reception and ceremony? It may work if you have a very small wedding, but why worry?
- You don't want the linens to be too loud or outshine the flowers.
- A mix of high and low arrangements will balance out the room.
- Low arrangements allow for a cozy and intimate affair.
- Whatever theme or color scheme you may choose, don't go over board. You don't want your quest for elegance to result in gaudiness.
- Make sure the florist decorates the buffet, not the hotel.

What's Not Elegant

- Tissue paper decorations such as bells
- Kazoos

- Bubbles
- Balloons
- Bows
- Paper plates, cups, and utensils
- Streamers

Let's Party—Fox-Trot and Photo Ops

PLANNING YOUR MUSIC AND PICTURES

If the music makes the party and the pictures preserve each hug, laugh, tear, and twirl on the dance floor, you'll want to guide the vendors you've chosen to make sure they don't miss a beat. You're probably excited about the people you picked to help create your dream wedding, and now you want to meet again to give some specific guidelines for what you want them to do at your wedding. This chapter will help you get the music and pictures you want.

Photography

Now that you've hired your photographer and your wedding day is getting closer, schedule another meeting so you can decide on a package and explain in more detail how you want the evening to go, and specifically who and what you want your photographer to capture. What should be the ratio of black-and-white to color photos, or of candid to portrait pictures? Don't assume your photographer will know what you like. Every couple is different. Some want 90 percent candid shots, while other couples want traditional portraits and maybe one roll of candids.

Spontaneous Moments

One of the luxuries of being a second-time bride is being able to do things differently. I wanted a photographer capable of capturing spontaneous moments. The photographer at my first wedding missed so many great shots. I remember charging across the dance floor to get him so he could photograph my little cousin dancing slow with his head nuzzled against my stomach. And the greatest picture of the bride-and-groom dance came from one of our guests.

Wedding Day Reflections

Some photographers we met had their logos tackily and prominently embossed at the bottom of each picture. We made sure ours didn't.

—Erin

Some photographers are comfortable with only posed pictures they can micromanage from the proper backdrop to the tilt of your head. One bride says she regrets hiring her photographer because he kept telling her *not* to smile, and she looks too serious in all of her wedding photos.

Here's a helpful bit of advice: Photographers are not all the same. I have several friends whose photographers happily gave them their entire set of proofs. Our photographer did not grant us our proofs. He wouldn't budge on this one. We were, however, invited to purchase them for $5 per photograph. I had 900-plus proofs! Needless to say, we don't have them.

We had the top package, which included unlimited coverage. Our photographer started in the afternoon, taking pictures behind the scenes of me getting ready. He got some great shots of me and

Bobby and of me alone—seeing each other for the first time in our wedding garb.

We met with our photographer a few times after we signed the contract. One meeting was our engagement photo session, which was part of our package. The break-the-ice shoot was helpful for all of us, and we had plenty of amazing outdoor pictures to choose from for our engagement announcement. At another meeting, we sat down with our photographer to discuss his role at our wedding. He asked what the most important parts of the wedding were to us, so he would know what to focus on. I told him the ceremony was very important to me, and I have to say, our ceremony pictures are phenomenal. We have close-ups of Bobby and me truly emotional, teary, and elated. The play-by-play of our ceremony was preserved on film. You can't stage those pictures, and if you try to take them beforehand you never get the same expressions. You can have the same gal, dress, and altar, but you'll see only that pensive or wide-eyed look while she's actually getting married.

> ## Second-Time Smarts
>
> Even if you are interested in all candids, take a few minutes and make a list of people your photographer should focus on. You'll be happier with the results when you have some wonderful pictures of your mom dancing with your son, or you and your best friend giggling during a private toast.

Lauran Wycoff of Lauran Wycoff Photography in Scottsdale, Arizona, knows the importance of meeting with your photographer in person before your wedding day, and making sure both parties understand what's expected of them. At her first wedding, the photographer whose book she previewed was not the one who shot her wedding. "There was major miscommunication, and the photographer didn't even show up until I was literally walking down the aisle. I was supposed to take pictures beforehand," she says. "I was a very unhappy bride for the rest of the day."

The "Must-Shoot" Photo List

Just as you did with the guest list, take some time to think about who's in and who's out. Keep in mind that if you ask people to arrive for posed pictures before the ceremony, they'll be inconvenienced because they have to get ready early and often will need to sit around watching until it is their turn. You can make a list of people you want captured on film and ask your photographer to snap a few pictures of them during the reception so they won't have to show up early. If you make sure your photographer knows who they are (someone can point them out), there should be no reason why you won't get your wish.

Even if you like the artistic look of black and white, I recommend instructing your photographer to take at least some photos in color. When you look back you'll see the colors of your flowers, the stunning place settings, your daughter's dress, the crimson leaves, the sunset. It's also nice to take some portraits. Yes, I know, the dreaded "point your toe, shoulders turned, chin up" shots seem to take forever and never come out looking like you. You can see the tension on everyone's faces. Even though they are often considered outdated for many of today's couples, your folks and grandparents will probably want a few standard family portraits. It doesn't hurt to pose for some with your immediate family. We did.

Professionally Speaking

To find a photographer in your area, contact the Professional Photographers of America, Inc., at www.ppa.com, or call 800-786-6277.

Our pre-ceremony photo session began only after Bobby had already seen me alone for the first time in my dress. We had a list for the photographer, and everyone was ready on time. I was happy to get these out of the way before the ceremony so we didn't have to miss any of our reception. (The posed pictures are my least favorite, but I guess I didn't want to buck tradition completely—

I did include some of them in my album.) The rest of the night we just got to "be" and didn't give a single thought to the camera. Our photographer followed us and the action, and the pictures came out amazing.

Every couple experiences precious moments during their wedding they never want to forget. My favorite moments were captured on film and they are now my favorite pictures: My father seeing me for the first time in my wedding gown. (It may be my second wedding, but I'm still his little girl.) The first time Bobby and I saw each other. Holding each other under the chuppah during our ceremony. Giddily leaving the ceremony together as man and wife. Hugging my parents after their toasts. Bobby and I laughing during the toasts. Dancing together all night long.

Photos You Can Skip

When deciding on what photos to *not* include, give the following shots some consideration.

> ## Second-Time Smarts
>
> If you have grandparents, definitely take pictures with them. It's also a good idea to get some of you alone with each of them and you and your husband with them. Your children will treasure these pictures for years to come.

TABLE SHOTS

Does anyone really look at the table shots? Yes, Mom says it's a nice way of seeing who was at your wedding, but I say there's always the video. Let the videographer pan the room for a few minutes. If your photographer is busy waiting around in front of table number three for Uncle Joe to get back from the bathroom and cousin Pam to come back from the bar, there is a problem: He's not following *you*. His camera is not on the two most important people—the bride and groom. It's your day, and your precious moments together could pass by if your photographer is spending chunks of time photographing each table.

BOUQUET AND GARTER TOSS

Are you even going to have them? Many second-time couples choose to leave them out. They are fun for the first wedding when you are younger and many of your friends are still single. Depending on your wedding and whether or not you feel these events are appropriate, you may not want to go with them—or take pictures of them if you do. At my second wedding, a bouquet toss would have consisted of maybe two friends. Most of our friends were attached, whether married, engaged, or happily living together.

GROUP SHOTS OF YOUR PARENTS
AND THEIR FRIENDS

I've seen rows of chairs lined up so the parents of the bride can get pictures taken with their dearest couples' friends. Such a group of 10 or so couples is nice for Mom and Dad, but again, the photographer is out in the hall and not shooting the party. It is impossible to accommodate all of your family members who want various configurations for their own personal albums. Perhaps a distant family member or friend would want to take these pictures for you.

CAKE-CUTTING

Our cake-cutting was more of a moment than an event. We didn't announce it. We just went to the cake table, cut the cake, and the photographer took pictures. We didn't even end up ordering any pictures of the cake-cutting. We just had so many candids of other moments that were more important to us. Unless you

Wedding Day Reflections

The things that were the most important to me in planning my second wedding were things I had overlooked the first time. I wanted a romantic video, so we searched until we found a vendor who truly knew how to capture the romance on film. We wanted the same in a photographer. Instead of the standard posed shots, we chose a photographer who had a more artistic, magazine-shoot flair.

—Leslie

really feel like the cake-cutting is a special event to you and your fiancé, don't feel obligated to have photos like this, just because they may have been a big deal at your first wedding.

Endless Wedding Party Shots

Remember the scene: a dozen bridesmaids and a dozen groomsmen crammed together on a platform with two little ring-bearers and a crying flower girl all crabby, hungry, and sweating, about to faint while the photographer asks them to lean in to the couple and then do a "crazy" picture where everybody makes a goofy face. Or the picture where the bridesmaids huddle around the groom and lean in with posed kisses, or the pictures where the entire wedding party gives a "thumbs up" sign or the bridesmaids all show a little leg. Such pictures are overrated. If you are having attendants, why not just take a couple of nice pictures, period.

Hiring the Videographer

Visit a few videographers, view their work, and you'll see that taping styles have changed since your last wedding. Technology has changed. Digital camcorders allow videographers to add color or change the focus. You can request your wedding taping on video or Digital Video Disc (DVD). Camcorders are smaller today and so are microphones. Big, bright lights and heavy equipment are no longer necessary.

Some videographers practice more artistic styles than their peers do. For example, their videos may include slow motion or black and white. The more imaginative videographers don't just make a tape of your wedding from beginning to end; they edit it and add special effects so it looks like something suited for the Sundance Film Festival. You can have your very own story-behind-your-wedding story. You

Questions to Ask Your Videographer

In addition to many of the questions you asked your photographer, you'll want to ask your videographer these questions:

- Will the camcorder stay in one spot all night? (I've been to the weddings where after a while the videographer just puts the camera on a tripod facing the dance floor and leaves it there.)

- How many cameras will be used?

- Will the videographer use photos of you and your groom growing up if you want him to?

- Will you be able to select the music?

- Will he or she let you review several of their recent wedding videos? (Be sure to listen to the video carefully to make sure you can hear what people are saying and that you can hear the music. You don't want it to look like people are just dancing to little voices in their heads.)

- Is their equipment up-to-date?

- What special services are offered?

- What special effects can be added?

- Who will videotape the wedding, and for how many hours? How many weddings has that individual done?

- Do they offer special wedding packages?

- Are there any extra charges?

- Will you receive the raw footage of the evening, or just an edited copy?

- Are extra copies included?

just need to figure out if you want more of an *MTV* or *Lifetime* look, and find the right videographer for the job. To find a videographer in your area, you can contact the Wedding and Event Videographers Association International (WEVA) at www.weva.com.

Some couples ask their videographers to cover the rehearsal dinner as well, and others have minimovies made: the story of how they met, complete with interview sessions and location shots of their favorite places. There are also second-time couples who choose to skip the video. Some want to spend more money on photos, and others say it's not a must because they don't see themselves popping in the wedding video and watching it.

Just as you gave your photographer instructions, be sure to let your videographer know who and what you'd like captured, and of course, what you don't want him to focus on. For example, if you don't want the microphone shoved in guests' faces, let your videographer know you'd rather your guests approach him if they want to speak on camera. If certain special dances are important to you, speak up. One groom had to ask his buddy to videotape a family huddle on the dance floor because the videographer wasn't paying attention. That was a special moment he wanted in his *professional* video, but at least the moment wasn't lost—it was captured on his friend's camcorder.

When to Toast

The music is playing and the camera is flashing, and it looks like you could be walking down the red carpet at a movie premiere. In the midst of the hoopla, you need to decide when to break the action for the toasts. You and your groom may have a special toast for each other, and you may want your children, best man, maid or matron of honor, and/or immediate family members to say a few words. I always love toasts at weddings. They are my favorite part. It's beautiful to a see a father describe his relationship with his child with such emotion.

You may decide to skip the toasts altogether. That's fine. You don't have to do the traditional toasts.

Places, Everyone

If you are happily abandoning the stadium-style seating you had at your first wedding, with bridesmaids and groomsmen displayed boy-girl facing the crowd, that's fine. You don't have to sit with your wedding party. Some couples choose to sit with their children. If you don't have children, you may want to honor your parents and siblings by seating them at the head table. And when I say "head table" I mean a table that is the same shape and on the same level as every other table in the room. If your families don't get along or if there is too much tension among sets of divorced parents, you and your groom can sit alone at a lovely table for two. This way, you won't be leaving anyone behind while you and your groom are making the rounds greeting your guests.

More Seating Tips

• Please don't try to seat your parents together if they are divorced or remarried in an effort to recapture that old we're-a-family-again feeling. Place divorced parents with people they are most comfortable with. You shouldn't split them up from their spouses, even if you don't like your stepparents.

• If you are doing assigned seating, make sure you don't assign your older guests smack in front of the speakers or the band. You don't want an earful about how the music is too loud.

Let's Do the Time Line

Fitting everything you want into your special night means sticking to a schedule. Unfortunately, you don't have your vendors—or guests—for an unlimited amount of time. The good news is that you and your groom don't have to watch the clock. You get to enjoy the flow of the evening. Your caterer or banquet manager will have a schedule of events so the food can be timed properly, but it's also a good idea to give a copy of the time line to the photographer, videographer, and band. Your wedding coordinator will surely have her bible of a list, but it's nice for the other vendors to be in sync. The bandleader or DJ is probably used to working with the catering staff, and will make sure your wedding doesn't miss a beat.

Here is one bride's sample schedule for her evening hotel wedding:

3:00 P.M.	Photo session begins
5:00 P.M.	Guests arrive
5:30 P.M.	Ceremony begins
6:00 P.M.	Reception begins
7:00 P.M.	Doors open
7:15 P.M.	Bride and groom introduced by band
7:20 P.M.	Bride and groom's first dance
7:30 P.M.	Blessing over the meal
7:35 P.M.	Dinner—first course; toasts given by [insert names here] and dancing
8:00 P.M.	Salad; additional toasts given by parents and bride and groom
8:40 P.M.	Entrée served
9:15 P.M.	Dessert served
9:55 P.M.	Cake-cutting
10:00 P.M.	Dancing
1:00 A.M.	Event concludes

• Avoid putting tables for your own family and friends on one side of the room and his on the other. You don't want a sense that there are two separate parties going on.

• If you are inviting children to your wedding, make sure there are adults sitting with them who are willing to supervise. You may think you are being considerate by putting the parents with their friends, but this may not go over well with the adults who become babysitters when seated next to children they don't know. Some kids need help cutting their food, and/or they may even be too shy to ask someone they don't know to pass the butter. An alternative is to have a kids' table with their parents at a nearby table.

Music

Did someone else pick the band at your first wedding? Was it the same band every other bride in the tri-county area used for her wedding? Did you know the group's song list and order by heart? In second weddings, music is always high on the priority list. Second-time couples won't settle for just any music. They want their music to be meaningful to them. And that may mean adding a little originality. If you are both rockabilly lovers, you may have hired your favorite rockabilly group. Or perhaps you chose a band well versed in many genres, including rock, soul, and R & B. Big Band music may be a way to connect multiple generations. Maybe you went for all Latin music. Latin bands are popular for weddings now, and swing bands have remained a wedding favorite.

How to Pick Your Beat

With your entertainment booked, now it's time to pick your beat. If you selected a versatile band or a DJ, you should have some options in the different kinds of music to offer. If you went with a salsa or a swing band, then you pretty much know what you are getting. But if the band plays everything from Motown to country, you'll want to go over their tapes and song lists again and let them know what types of music you want them to play more of or less of—or not at all.

If you love show tunes, then let the bandleader or DJ know so they have several in their lineup. Some bands rely on playing the same songs for every wedding, and it gets old. If you're tired of "We Are Family" and "I Will Survive," talk to your band about changing their list. Explain that you expect certain songs to be played at your wedding. Just be sure they are not left with too many songs they are not used to playing. Many wedding bands have their lists perfected to the point where they could give Gloria Gaynor a run for her money. At our wedding, several of our requests were ignored. Make sure your entertainers listen to you. I highly recommend handing them a specific song list so they can't say they "never got the fax with your requests," or some other excuse. Your song list also serves as instructions in writing for your band or DJ so they know exactly what you want. It actually can make things easier because the DJ or band can just follow your lead instead of guessing whether you are Top 40 people or classic rock fans. It's always good to avoid any breakup songs or songs about wrongin' your man or woman, or anything with negative lyrics.

You don't have to freak out if there is a song or two that was played at your first wedding. Trust me, no one will remember, and you don't want to tell the band that four hours' worth of their best songs are off limits. However, there is one exception: Do not play the song that was your first dance with your first husband. Even if you had no intention of using it for "your" song with your fiancé (thank goodness), it still should not be played at all—it's just too creepy!

In general, it's good to have a mix of genres and eras so you don't alienate any guests. Some old standbys are always great for weddings. For example, Frank Sinatra songs manage to bridge all generations. Your friends, your parents' friends, and your great aunts and uncles will enjoy dipping one another to "Fly Me to the Moon" and "The Way You Look Tonight."

Music is personal—as personal as your relationship with your fiancé. A song that is beautiful and meaningful to you may be a joke to another couple. Definitely make a "don't even think about it" song list. The list can include specific artists or songs you do not want played at your wedding. An example might look like this (changed to your liking—or disliking—of course):

Do not play the following groups or artists:

Celine Dion

Mariah Carey

Kiss

Please play anything by:

Earth Wind & Fire

The Rolling Stones

Commodores

Van Morrison

Temptations

Dave Matthews Band

U2

Tony Bennett

Frank Sinatra

Sarah McLachlan

You need to give your band or DJ a schedule of events for the night: when the cake will be cut; who is giving the toasts, and when; how many courses will be served, and when. Also tell them whether you want music and dancing during the meals or dessert, and whether there are any special dances or traditions that need to be honored. We didn't want any dances like line dances, conga lines, the Hokey Pokey, and certainly not the "Chicken Dance." But don't be afraid to throw a few quirky tunes into the mix. Wedding coordinators and music reps say the unexpected is always a treat at weddings.

You Can Dance If You Want To

Don't let anyone tell you that you don't get a first dance. Every couple deserves a first dance dedicated just to them. The stress of the wedding planning, the ceremony, and the guest-greeting is over, and now for the first time, you can take a breath and look into your husband's eyes as you circle as one around the dance floor. These moments are often some of the best candid shots for the photographer. Couples laughing, kissing, and stroking each other's hair or cheek always end up as framers. You are in the moment. Before he has to share his bride with the rest of the party, he gets the first dance with you.

Your love song with your man is *your* love song. I won't laugh and neither will your guests. Be true to your relationship and pick that campy tune you sing privately to one another. You want your bandleader to croon your favorite Barry Manilow tune? Just let him know beforehand so he's prepared. We wanted a Bee Gees tune, "How Deep Is Your Love?" Not exactly the most in-demand song at parties, but, nevertheless, we wanted it played at our wedding. That didn't happen, though. (More on my interesting band experience later.)

Don't worry if your favorite song is a fast song. You can ask someone you know who plays guitar to do a slower acoustic version of the song. Don't assume that because your song is not popular, "out there," or not on their playlist, the band won't play it. Many bands will happily learn your song. You just need to provide them with a tape or the sheet music. If you must dance to your favorite REM or U2 song, ask your band if they will learn it. For my brother's wedding, the band learned an Aerosmith tune so he could dance with his beautiful bride to his favorite song. (The musicians also learned his favorite football team's fight song for the couple's grand entrance as husband and wife.)

Be sure to really listen to the words of your song. No matter how beautiful the melody or how sensational the singer's voice, or how emotional or passionate the performance, the song for your first dance must not be sad or about breaking up. Skip songs that remind you of something negative. Remember that in the movie *The Wedding Planner*, Jennifer Lopez's character says couples who pick "I Honestly Love You" are doomed.

It's a good idea to save some songs for when it's just the two of you. Even if Marvin Gaye's "Sexual Healing" is your special song because it was playing the night you met, you might want to select something else for your first dance so your children and guests don't feel uncomfortable.

It's All in the Details

- Reconfirm your dates and times with your vendors a week before the wedding. It won't hurt to call two weeks before the wedding as well.

- In addition to song instructions, let the band or DJ know what type of music is acceptable for "nondancing" time. If you don't want to leave the cocktail hour or dining music up to the DJ, explain that you'd like "light jazz" or "classical CDs" played during dinner. Perhaps you want to hire an a cappella group to sing your favorite Motown songs during dinner or the cocktail hour.

- Make sure you and your entertainer are in sync with lighting. You don't want to spend your precious time and money creating

Fun Reception Ideas

- View your wedding from a child's eyes: Have your kids take Polaroid pictures of guests as they arrive. The pictures can be put into a scrapbook afterward.

- Bag the guest book: Set out a silver bowl with small cards so guests can write a special note to you.

- Honor all the grandparents in the room by having your bandleader invite them on the dance floor for their own medley of songs.

the ultimate mood lighting with candlelight, only to have your DJ come in and set up strobe lights and a disco ball (and some sound effects to boot).

- Your DJ or bandleader *must* properly pronounce the name of each person he will announce or introduce. Meet with him during the week of your wedding to go over each person's name phonetically. Our bandleader didn't want to meet first, and it was our loss. We should have demanded it in our contract. He pronounced half of the names wrong and even forgot to call up one of the matrons of honor. He was lazy and in the middle of moving or something (at least that's what his rep said), and it showed. He wasn't prepared, and that sent a message to me that he didn't care about our wedding.

- He also announced the father/daughter dance when I was out of the room. How hard is it to scan the room first for the woman in the white dress? He announced the blessing of the challah bread when I was in the bathroom. My great-uncle Sonny, who flew in for my wedding, was given the honor and I missed it. The bandleader also hurt my in-laws when he called my father-in-law's name and left out his wife. I specifically explained that they were to be announced together.

• If you don't want your bandleader or DJ to emcee the evening, you should make that clear. Sometimes it goes with the territory unless they are instructed not to make announcements over the microphone. For example, if you want the catering staff to quietly ask guests to make their way to the ballroom rather than have the bandleader announce it, inform both the entertainment and the catering staff.

You now have the music and photos covered. You can look forward to an amazing reception. Get ready to boogie!

Suit or Sheath?

WHAT TO WEAR

Can I wear a gown? How about a veil? Dare I wear white? Despite how common second weddings are today, these questions still puzzle second-time brides, who wonder if they are destined to don a cocktail dress in order to avoid looking like a first-time virgin bride. Can they wear a train? Where can they shop? Will bridal salons shun them?

Let's get a couple of things out of the way. First, you will be welcomed by bridal salons, department stores, and dress designers. You are part of a large group—about 46 percent of all marriages involve at least one person who has been previously married.

Second, you *can* wear a wedding gown, and you *can* wear white. My goodness, you're not Elizabeth Taylor. It's your second wedding, not your eighth.

I've read articles that said second-time brides should *not* call attention to themselves by wearing veils or trains and instead should don a cocktail suit and hat. One wedding etiquette tome says women older than age 40 do not usually look their best in wedding dresses. It offers options such as evening gowns, tea-length dresses, and dressy suits. (Mind you, this was the updated version of the book!) I wonder if the author saw second-time bride Andie MacDowell in *In Style Weddings*, modeling pages of wedding regalia? She even wore her strapless Vera Wang ball gown—with train—for the cover. She looked phenomenal.

If you have nice skin you can get away with a strapless, scoop back, or sleeveless gown. Why not highlight your assets? Let's be honest. Many women in their 40s are in great shape and probably happier with their figures than they were in their 20s. Just don't wear a dress that is too tight, too short, or too similar to your first wedding gown.

Where to Shop?

Anywhere. Department stores (the bridal salon and in evening wear), dress boutiques, bridal salons, consignment stores, vintage or antique dress boutiques, or the juniors section at department stores (prom and holiday dresses are stylish and reasonable). You can also shop online at sites such as www.BridesMade.com, where you can find designer samples and manufacturers' overstocks. This site is also a great outlet for reselling wedding gowns and bridesmaids' dresses. Some brides also have great luck with borrowing. One bride I know accepted her friend's wedding dress and just reworked the design a bit. She was relieved not to pay for a second wedding dress.

Be sure you know the store policy before you buy any gown. Be cautious if you go to a bridal discount house. The gowns often are on final sale, and if you receive the gown in poor condition, you won't be able to return it.

It's easier for second-time brides to shop for gowns. You have many options and you can bypass the frilly 21-year-old virginal look of the high-necked, over-the-top pearl-encrusted lace and tulle gown. And I'm guessing you'll also pass on the elbow-length gloves, 10-foot train, and cathedral veil.

Finding Your Style

Be open-minded. Don't get set on a certain dress. Even if you don't love a gown on the hanger, try it on. It may look incredible on you. And if the dress you loved in the magazine isn't attractive on you, move on. There are plenty of exceptional dresses available, and you will find a gown that makes you look wonderful.

Fortunately, after decades of trying on jeans and bathing suits in tiny dressing rooms with unflattering lighting, you know that choosing a flattering gown will be a cinch. You know your body. If you are bottom-heavy (often pegged a pear or triangle by fashion mags), you know to avoid straight skirts. You want to draw attention upward to a beautiful neckline or elongated waistline. If you are petite, you know a wide skirt will make you look shorter.

Wedding dresses come in an array of styles, with variations in everything from the neckline to the hemline. Your upper-body options alone include halter, scoop, V neck, square neck, sweetheart, and off-the-shoulder. You can have straps or go strapless. If you want sleeves, there are cap, short, three-quarter, and long fitted sleeves.

Here are some common silhouettes:

Empire. The fitted bodice is great for small-busted women because the waistline hits below the bust. It's also a roomy fit for pregnant women.

A-line. It's flattering on most figure types, with a fitted top, and the skirt flares out in the shape of an A.

Ball gown. It's romantic and poufy—fitted at the waist with a big skirt often made of several layers of fabric. It's flattering on many body shapes.

Sheath. This style is unstructured and made in flowing fabrics that tend to be clingy and sexy. It's a good look for thin, petite, or curvy shapes. If you don't want to accentuate your curves, this isn't the best style for you.

Second-Time Shopping Tips

- Don't pay too much attention to trends.

- Do bring the shoes and bra you will wear to your wedding. The bridal salon staffers repeated this mantra to me several times before scheduling my first fitting. Even a slight variation in heel height or fit of your bra can change the way your gown looks on your body.

- If you are ordering a gown, tell the salesperson that your wedding date is earlier than the actual date. That extra cushion of time is helpful if they fall behind. You want your gown finished before your wedding, with plenty of time to spare for alterations.

- Try dancing around the dressing room at your fittings. Can you bend over without your breasts falling out? If someone tall greets you, will they see down your gown? Can you raise your arms freely? Can you bend and twist without worrying about ripping your dress? Does it stay in place? Can you get around in heels without your dress weighing you down?

- Don't shop with a group. You don't need everyone from your matron of honor to your coworkers chiming in on which dresses they like best. Bring along a trusted pal with good taste—someone who will be honest.

• Do check with bridal salons to find out when gowns go on sale.

• *Do not under any circumstances* wear your dress from your first wedding, no matter how expensive it was. It's off limits—even if you alter it, adorn it, or dye it!

And You Thought You Couldn't Wear a Sheath!

Ever since you saw photographs of style icon Carolyn Bessette Kennedy wearing a sexy sheath when she married John F. Kennedy Jr., you figured women had to be 6 feet tall and built like a beanpole to carry off the clingy, nightgown-like style. But it's a myth that you need to be stick-thin or hipless to wear a sheath. "Bias-cut sheath dresses look beautiful on an hour-glass figure," says Amy Michelson (www.amymichelson.com), the new Dress Designer of the Year (2001) Couture Bridal Awards, who has dressed many celebrities in evening wear, including Michelle Pfeiffer, Kim Basinger, and Halle Berry.

When Amy started designing bias-cut sheaths for weddings, she filled a need for women who don't want princess wedding gowns—many of whom are second-time brides. Amy says 20 percent of her customers are second-time brides. "They want to feel like the bride without looking silly or like the cake-topper princess brides," says Amy.

Professionally Speaking

There is not as much separation as there used to be between what a woman wants to look like in her daily life and what she wants to look like on her wedding day. She doesn't want to turn into someone else. Today, it's more acceptable to look fashionable instead of just a bride.

—Amy Michelson,
Los Angeles dress designer

The sheath has always been an elegant choice. Amy accents the simple sheath in a modern way with traditional beading, crystals, and tulle. She's sold her elegant "Moet" dress—a bias-cut strapless

silk chiffon sheath dress with Swarovski pearls and a built-in bra—
to women ranging from ages 22 to 60. "The bias-cut sheath is timeless, classic, and it has a flow and softness to it," she says. "When a
dress has an evening-wear influence to it, it has sophistication."

But white clingy silk? Already you're thinking cellulite alert,
right? Amy says not to worry about being too revealing. She
double-lines her dresses so cellulite isn't visible.

My Dress Hunt

It just so happened that right after I got engaged I had a trip
planned to New York City with my mom. Any newly engaged
woman plunked in the center of fashion is going to go a little overboard. I was no exception. I wanted to explore the dresses the city
had to offer. I figured I'd see what spoke to me. I knew I wanted
something different, but I didn't know *how* different. The dress I
wore in my first wedding was an ecru-colored ball gown with a fitted bodice, sweetheart neck, and long sleeves. Suddenly, I found
myself in the middle of Manhattan trying on antique lace dresses at
one boutique and a two-piece rather wild Italian design with pink
and white flowers sprouting out of it at another. (It was definitely
something only a second-timer would consider.) Then, several
swanky boutiques later, we were set on having a very simple, long
strapless gown custom-made. The sample looked smashing, but
each dress was made to order. I guess we got a bit carried away.
What were we thinking? Mothers and daughters can't help themselves; mention the words *wedding* and *dress* and they lose all control.
We eventually came to our senses, realizing that the idea of flying
to New York for all of my fittings would be an absurd expense. It
was back to the drawing board when I got home.

Originally I thought I'd just purchase a simple cocktail dress. I
didn't want anything "bridey." Then I started looking at the bridal

salons and found a white A-line wedding gown complete with beading on the bodice. It was everything I didn't want, and it was perfect. My mom convinced me to pick the gown because it was so classic, so Grace Kelly. She absolutely loved it on me. I'm glad I listened to her.

My gown was fabulous, but I needed to make it my own. I had the tank-style straps removed and left the halter straps, a look that was much more flattering for my bone structure. The dress was cut low in the back and I didn't wear a bra, but the beaded top was tight enough that I could dance without a problem. Since I really wanted something more evening gown than princess bride, I had the seamstress chop off the train. I knew from experience that it's not fun dancing at your own wedding with pounds of fabric bustled to your backside.

I didn't wear a veil. Instead, I had my hair pulled back in a sophisticated chignon accented with tiny white flowers. Not wearing a veil meant my hair didn't look like moist pieces of straw hanging from my head due to random tugs on the veil with each guest's hug.

Don't be afraid to change your gown. I know one bride who added cap sleeves to her gown, and another who bought a wedding dress at the end of the season for $150 and spent an additional $240 adding a detachable train and lowering the scooped back.

Rules? What Rules?

Popular wedding lore tells future brides to choose their wedding dress based on the formality of their event. But why limit yourself? Let's say you are having a country elegant wedding with guests wearing anything but jeans. Does that mean you can't look like the bride and wear a beautiful wedding gown? No.

You don't have to wear a spaghetti-strap minidress and flip-flops just because your wedding is at the beach. Of course, if you want to, go ahead. But you're the bride, so you can wear the gown even if your guests are in sundresses and khakis. I may have every fashionista bridal designer dropping their mouths at this declaration, but that's okay. I know you're not afraid to break the rules. *Please* wear what you feel most comfortable and beautiful in and don't worry about coordinating your material or style with your bridesmaids, tablecloths, reception site, season, or anything else for that matter.

And if you want to wear a simpler dress, you don't have to wear a cocktail-length dress. Simple doesn't mean it can't be formal. You can wear a long dress. You can be the most dressed-up person there. You are the bride!

According to Beth Reed Ramirez of *Bride Again*, a blusher veil is the only taboo item for second-time brides because it represents virginity. Some wedding folks go a step further and say brides should refrain from donning any type of veil or train because all of them are symbols of virginity and worn by women who have never been married. It's hard to keep it all straight. Don't worry about wedding etiquette that was written eight decades ago. Make your own rules. Wear what you want. I've talked to many brides who opted to wear a veil. It's a personal choice.

There are really only three things to consider:

1. What will make you feel beautiful?
2. What will make you look like the bride?
3. What would your groom like to see? (He may dream of his bride walking toward him wearing a princess bridal gown.)

"The old rigid rules need to be thrown away," says Diane Forden, editor in chief of *Bridal Guide* magazine. "The rules dictated that second-time brides shouldn't wear white or a gown with a train, but today's second-time brides are too independent, smart, and savvy to adhere to stuffy rules."

Bridal Fashion

Wedding dresses are sexier and softer today. You won't feel like you are trying to look 20. Gowns today are designed for a woman's figure and spunk, not her age. According to Diane Forden, dress designers are all creating gowns that work for second- and third-time brides. "The silk bias-cut gown is very glamorous and elegant, and there are a lot of beautiful strapless and mermaid-style dresses," she says. "There are also dresses with stunning beading and embroidery." You don't have to spend thousands of dollars on a gown detailed with embroidery—she says there are gorgeous gowns from manufacturers that don't charge a fortune.

The best dress is the dress that looks best on you. It doesn't matter if it was inexpensive. If it flatters your figure and you feel beautiful in it, who cares about the price? No one is going to ask how much your dress cost. Just make sure the gown is well made and won't fall apart. You don't want loose seams or beads hanging the minute someone hugs you.

Your gown can be any color, from bordeaux to black, peach, or plum. Whether you see yourself as modern or romantic, earthy or ethereal, there are many styles you can consider. Here are some general looks I've seen lately:

- Wrap dresses
- Slip dresses with embroidered cardigans
- Crepe gowns with asymmetrical necklines
- White satin tanks with matching A-line skirts
- Silk jersey boatneck dresses
- Coatdresses trimmed in fur
- Embroidered netting gowns with spaghetti straps
- Nude sheaths and strapless gowns with lace overlays

Hollywood Glamour – The Second Time Around

Amy E. Goodman, an editor at *In Style Weddings* magazine, shares her expert observations of celebrity second-time brides:

1. *There are no set rules for second-time brides.* Several celebrity brides chose to approach their second weddings as traditionalists donning white, with full gowns and veils, from Andie MacDowell's princess-like silk duchesse satin gown and Mel Harris's tulle veil to Julia Roberts' tiara and Lauren Holly's cream Escada sheath gown with lace overlay.

2. *A bride's style should be her own.* Whether it is her first or second marriage, she should wear a dress that is comfortable and expresses who she is. In her second wedding, Brooke Shields went tropical, wearing fresh flowers in her hair and streamlining her dress to something simple, sleek, and elegant.

3. *A nonwhite dress can be stunning.* Actress Elizabeth Perkins donned a bronze, off-the-shoulder duchesse satin Richard Tyler dress with a hand-embroidered bodice and small train for her second wedding. Natalie Cole wore an off-the-shoulder gray-and-lavender beaded chiffon dress by J&M Costumers.

If you simply can't decide, don't fret! You live in a time when gowns are reversible and have detachable components. You don't have to pick just one look. You can walk down the aisle in a vision of white and then flip your dress inside out and wear black lace for the reception. I've seen strapless silk gowns with illusion body suits underneath so you can have long sleeves for the ceremony and bare skin for the party. You can even zip off your long skirt and train and dance all night in a taffeta minidress. Since second-time brides have more freedom to wear what they want, designers also have additional freedom. "I can get more creative with second weddings. The brides are more relaxed," says Bryan K. Osburn of Bryan K. Osburn Bridal Collection in Charlotte, North Carolina, who designs custom wedding gowns and mother-of-the bride evening wear. For weddings, Bryan has designed everything from pale green and ice blue gowns to platinum and chocolate brown. He's designed evening wear for celebrities including Cindy Crawford, Diana Ross, and Patti LaBelle.

"Styles that are popular for the second-time bride are nontraditional evening-wear looks that fit closer to the body and don't have a lot of fabric in the skirts or a lot of bridal beaded laces," he says. There are clingier fabrics today that were not available 10 years ago. Gone are the stiff fabrics, heavy lace, and big sleeves.

If you're going the custom route, make sure you have the proper undergarments and that you know your price points, Bryan says. Be sure your designer answers all of your questions about fabrics and dress delivery.

So What Do Second-Timers Really Wear?

My gown is ivory with very little decoration except for pearls on top of the bodice. It's a classic look. My beloved is wearing black tails with an ivory vest and shirt.

—JANICE

My husband's mom was horrified that I chose to wear a white gown. She's a conservative traditional Southern woman and thought that wasn't proper. But she was so moved at the wedding and loved my gown. I wanted to wear white for my husband. I wanted him to have the full "bride" effect on our wedding day.

—CHRISTINE

For my beach wedding, I found a celadon green dress at Ann Taylor. My husband wore a Hawaiian shirt and khakis.

—MARLA

My dress at my first wedding was poufy and lacy with a veil. At my second wedding I wore a simple and sexy strapless dress. It was very tight all the way down with a very small train. I didn't wear a veil but I made hairpins with pearls and beads, and they were beautiful. They sell in stores for $350 to $700 for a set of five, and I made mine for under $30!

—JESSICA

For my first wedding I wore a very traditional dress with long sleeves, a big tulle skirt, and a cathedral-length veil. For my second wedding I still wanted to wear a dress. My husband wanted me to wear a veil for the walk down the aisle, so I did. I chose a Renaissance-style gown in a beautiful golden cham-

Oops, Did We Forget the Groom?

Chances are your man owns a tux. If your wedding is formal he'll wear it. Encourage him to splurge on a new shirt, shoes, and socks. If your wedding is not black tie, he can buy a dark suit or wear one of his own. If it's a casual wedding he might opt for a shirt and pants and skip the tie. You know him best. What would he be happiest in?

The groom can let his personality show with details such as cuff links, shoes, or hats. One groom insisted on wearing his cowboy boots. An avid airplane lover wore silver airplane studs on his tuxedo shirt. Another groom honored his Scottish heritage by sporting a kilt. "It was two shades of purple to match my dress, which was purple and royal blue velvet," says his wife, Dianne. "David's attire even influenced his 'best man,' who is a woman. Since he wore a skirt, she wore pants!"

pagne silk organza. It was strapless with beautiful stitching in a floral pattern. It had a corset look to the front, and I had definite cleavage showing. I'm older now, but young enough to look amazing in a wedding dress. Because it was my second wedding, I figured, why not go for it? I never would have worn that for my first wedding, but I am also more comfortable with myself now that I'm older. I look at it like I was so lucky that I got to wear a bridal gown and dress like a princess twice!

—CAROLYN

I didn't see any reason not to wear a veil. I still wanted to be the bride for my husband. I wore an elegant two-piece ivory satin fitted top and A-line floor-length skirt.

—MICHELE

I had my dress made. My mother-in-law and I designed it, which was a nice bonding experience. It was an ivory satin slip dress with a sheer overlay with lace trim. It was kind of vintage-looking and extra special because it was our creation.

—BETH

I flaunted convention and wore a "traditional" dress for both my first and second wedding. The first was off the shoulder, straight, with a detachable short train. I wore an off-the-shoulder gown with a full skirt to my second wedding (very Cinderella and not like me at all, but I liked it!). I wore a headpiece for both weddings—I never liked the whole veil thing. Of course I was living with both men before I married them, but I still wore white!

—KELLY

My dress is a butter-colored, V-neck Italian silk dress that looks like the dress Cruella wears in 101 Dalmations. It's fitted with jeweled buttons straight down to the tulip bottom. It has beaded French cuffs with a giant *rhinestone and the collar stands up like a vampire's, with whale bones. It was made by a couture designer. Instead of a veil, I wore cream-colored ostrich feathers and jeweled pins in my hair with a cream-colored "net" that stopped at my nose.*

—ANNE

You're No Registering Rookie

CREATING A REGISTRY LIST BEYOND CHINA AND CUTLERY

You know about registering. Chances are you registered for your own bridal showers and baby showers, and you've been to showers for your friends and family. You know Waterford from Wedgwood and Calphalon from Cuisinart. You're no registering rookie. But one little question lingers. Is it okay to register the second time around?

Yes! You absolutely can and should register. Your closest friends and family will want to honor your marriage, and many will do so with a wedding present. Giving a gift is a way of wishing you a bright future. People who love and care for you will give you gifts no matter which wedding this is for you.

If you are inviting guests who were also at your first wedding, they don't have to give you gifts again, but they probably will. You might as well select things you like. Don't feel bad about it. They are giving you a present as a token of their love. And if your dear friend gets married for the second time, you will surely give her a gift too. It's just what good friends do.

Of course, you don't want to get carried away and register for incredibly expensive pieces at Tiffany & Co., without offering lower-priced alternatives at other stores. It's important to give your guests a choice of several places. Make sure at least two of the stores are on the Web so your guests won't have to run around to three different stores looking for a specific toaster oven. And if your families are in different cities, you might want to register at a few different stores in each location.

Don't rule out the national chains or department stores. They make gift-buying easier, especially for your out-of-town guests. Many people like to see what they are buying for you. The national stores also have Web sites so people don't have to go to the store if they don't want to. They can pay with a credit card online and the gift is shipped to you. A bonus for you with many department stores and chains is that they will give you a discount for remaining items on your registry. When we registered at a local department store, we received 10 percent off the rest of our registry items for one year after our wedding.

Depending on your situation, registering for some new things may make perfect sense. Maybe your ex ran off with all of your wedding gifts and you have little more than a futon and a cat to your name. Or maybe you didn't want anything in your place that reminded you of your ex, so you sold the crystal and the china. Or maybe you didn't receive gifts at your first wedding. Perhaps you eloped. Even if you have a house full of grown-up things, your new spouse may want new things that you selected together instead of stuff that's hanging around from a shower your ex's aunts hosted years ago. Janice, 39 and a mother of three, registered for the typical "bridal" items such as dishes, appliances, and sheets. "All of the stuff I had was old and needed to be replaced anyway, and as for my husband, his ex had pretty much taken everything (the wedding gifts and furniture) before they ever went to court," she says. "So registering really meant a fresh start for both of us. We wanted things that were ours."

Registering Today

If you haven't bought a wedding or shower gift lately, you're in for a surprise. Bridal registry has gone beyond the stores keeping a tally of your likes and dislikes. Your registry now will be in cyberspace if the retailer has a Web site. Registries also have expanded to stores that traditionally never had them, such as home improvement stores and artsy boutiques. In addition, you can register for items beyond the basic kitchen essentials. How about luggage, music, or books? You can register for computer and electronic equipment or gardening tools and sporting gear. You can decorate the house or enjoy your hobbies with your gifts. Almost anything you want is within registry range. Believe it or not, couples even register with travel agents for honeymoons and with banks for a mortgage!

It's a whole different playing field now. Prior to your first wedding you may not even have had a home of your own. This time you know what you need and want for your home. You've developed your tastes. If you need linens, you don't want just any linens; you'd like 300-thread-count sheets. You can register at a small specialty linens boutique for all of your luxe boudoir accessories. If that's what you really want, maybe several of your friends will pool their resources to give you a gift.

You also can register at unique little gift boutiques and galleries. Many small shops will keep a list of your favorite items even if they don't have a formal bridal registry system. Just let them know you have friends and family who may be coming in and asking what you selected.

I registered at a store in a woman's basement. She sold only Judaica, and you had to make an appointment. It obviously wasn't as convenient as being able to go online to purchase a gift, but only my immediate family made the trip there anyway because the items were very special to me. At my first wedding I didn't pick out any Judaica. I was so overwhelmed with trying to pick out basics like dishes and pots and pans that I didn't have the time to focus on the smaller, more personal or decorative items. It was important to me to select some special Jewish pieces for my home with Bobby. I knew I'd have them for the holidays, and when I wasn't using them, they'd look beautiful displayed on our shelves.

Whether you want furniture or tools, crystal or cutlery, you'll find a plethora of places that offer bridal registries today, such as:

Bed Bath & Beyond	REI
Crate & Barrel	Restoration Hardware
Fortunoff	Sears
Home Depot	Smith & Hawkin
Neiman Marcus	Target
Pier 1 Imports	Tiffany & Co.
Pottery Barn	Williams-Sonoma

Items you may not have registered for the first time:

Bikes	Luggage
Books	Mortgage
Camera equipment	Music
Computers	Plants
Couches	Sleeping bags
Gardening equipment	Sporting gear
Grill	Tents
Honeymoon	Tools
Lamps	Wine

Registering 101

You may not have had the opportunity or the desire to register on-line when you got married the first time. There now are sites designed just for bridal registering, and individual stores have their own registries. If you still like the old-fashioned way of seeing and touching an item in person, that's fine. Just be sure to have an appointment in advance. Maybe an evening after work will work best for both of you. Don't even think about trying a department store on a Saturday. You'll have a splitting headache before you make it down the first aisle. Registering is always more fun when you don't feel rushed and there isn't a crowd.

> ## Professionally Speaking
>
> I think registering is one of the best things that's ever happened. It's even more important with a second-time bride, because it's not as easy to know what she needs.
> —Beth Reed Ramirez, editor of *Bride Again*

Prior to my first wedding, I was clueless about registering. In all honesty, the word *stemware* wasn't exactly in my vocabulary. Registering was completely stressful. I didn't know what I liked, and it all became a blur after a while. I remember having no clue as to what I wanted. I actually asked our registry consultant at the department store what colors she liked, and I believe she picked out our towels. My second wedding registering experience was way different. Bobby and I knew we could make perfectly fine decisions without assistance.

Bobby, though a first-time groom, was a natural, and assumed his role as most grooms do: scanner-gun guy. Men suddenly get giddy about gifts because they get to shop without spending a penny and with a gadget in hand zapping items along the way. You send him to register for a coffee grinder, and all of a sudden you hear "Honey, we need a waffle iron, don't we?" Twenty minutes later you get a printout of your registry and you find a slew of items you weren't plan-

Other Brides Are Doing It

- "I was shocked that people gave us wedding presents. I didn't think they would, but I was so touched when they did. It showed that they truly supported our union." —Becky

- "We registered at Home Depot. We love Home Depot. We got everything on the list: drills, saws, ladders, toolboxes, gardening tools, shrubbery, a gas grill, and tiles to redo our kitchen!" —Cheryl

- "Our registry reflects our interests. We entertain a lot so we registered for two sets of everyday dishes and lots of extra serving pieces." —Anne

- "I agonized at first about whether or not to register. We both lived on our own and had everything we needed, but people were still asking what we wanted. I thought it would be better to register so our friends could get us things we liked." —Carolyn

- "Registering for my second wedding was not strange. My weddings were seven years apart and I think registering is fun. I'm a big fan of getting stuff." —Bob

ning to register for. Your hubby-to-be went a little zap-happy and signed you on for three sets of dishes with matching gravy boats. Fortunately, what makes the list can be deleted from the list.

Where Are You Registered?

Let people come to you and ask where you are registered. It's not polite to offer the information. Your guests will have no problem learning where you are registered; word of mouth has worked for years. If you'd prefer money, your family can spread the word. If a guest approaches you it's fine to be honest and say you're trying to save toward a new house or for your honeymoon, but don't ask anyone for money.

If you're confused about how to handle the word *gift* on your wedding invitations, here's a simple tip: omit it. Any mention of gifts on a wedding invitation is considered tacky. And though you may not want your guests to purchase gifts for you, stating "no gifts" on the invitations isn't any better. A reference like that assumes you're getting gifts and takes the focus away from the fact that you are inviting them to join you on your wedding day.

A Different Approach

If you are marrying a first-time groom, his family and friends will certainly want to give him a wedding gift. If you and your groom don't want your guests to purchase gifts for you, you can ask your guests to give to a charity instead. Guests can donate any dollar amount they like, and you will know their money is going toward a cause you care about. You can even ask that donations be made in lieu of gifts for any pre-wedding showers or parties.

You can pick the charity of your choice, local or national, and you can even set up a charity of your own. You might want the money to go toward finding a cure for cancer or helping inner-city kids receive school supplies. You decide on the cause. You can research charities on the Internet at sites like www.giveforchange.com and www.MarriedForGood.com.

SARAH'S STORY

We just couldn't allow people to give us gifts. Instead, if they wished to do something, we asked them to give a contribution to our favorite charity. The charity got $5,000 as a result of our wedding, and people could feel good about honoring us while helping a worthy cause (and getting a tax deduction). I personally don't feel that people should expect gifts for a second wedding, particularly if it is relatively close to the first wedding and many of the guests are the same.

Second-Time Showers—Yes or No?

You *can* have a shower. If your guests are mostly new friends, neighbors, or coworkers, it's not an issue that you've been married before. They will be giving you gifts for the first time. If you've stayed close to your old friends, you may feel a little funny including women who were at the shower for your first wedding. If you want to celebrate your engagement with these friends, you can have a get-together without gifts. The invitation won't have the word *shower* on it because whether it's an evening party for couples or a luncheon for ladies, "shower" means "bring gifts."

My mother's close friends insisted on hosting a shower for my second wedding even though they also did for my first. I felt they had already done enough for me, so I told my mother I didn't want a shower. They ended up hosting a beautiful tea for me at a gorgeous hotel, and I was able to celebrate my upcoming wedding with my friends without having to accept gifts.

Wedding Day Reflections

I had more pre-wedding celebrations for my second wedding than for my first. My friends threw me a big shower and an engagement party. I didn't even have an engagement party for my first wedding. I didn't feel like I deserved gifts again, but my friends convinced me to register. It helped to realize that it was simply their way of expressing their love and congratulations, and the most gracious thing I could do was to accept their gifts and be thankful for their love and generosity.

—Christine

Because Bobby had never been married, his family and friends wanted to host a bridal shower. It wasn't awkward because I hadn't received gifts from them before, and I knew they all wanted to give Bobby gifts.

I know people probably told you in the past that it's okay for your shower invitations to list where you are registered, but it's not. Your friends don't want to open an invitation and then have a handful of store cards fall to the floor. If they want to know where you are registered, they will call the hosts, your mother, or your bridesmaids, or ask you directly. I know you are not in charge of the shower, but you can tell your hostesses how you feel, and they will certainly honor your wishes.

Second-Time Smarts

Try to register during the week and avoid Saturdays if possible. Register for more items than you think you'll receive and register for gifts in a wide range of prices, so your guests have choices.

As your wedding approaches, update your registry. You may receive most of your items at your shower, and you want people to have options if they want to buy you a wedding gift.

HALLIE'S STORY

I never registered for expensive gifts the first time—just practical things. I did register before my second wedding and it felt awkward getting fine china, silver, and crystal, but only because I don't come from a culture where we give gifts. My family gives money. I grew up in a practical family where we did not have separate dishes for holidays, so it was difficult for me to say, yes, I do want fine china and to pick out the pattern. I still have a bit of a lump in my throat when I look at the Lenox boxes. But on the flip side, Ken and I gave away all of the things we had from our former lives—appliances, dishes, glassware—everything that had the memory of another person attached. It was tough to give away perfectly useful stuff, but we felt it was necessary.

Renting Rides and Rooms

PLANNING YOUR TRANSPORTATION AND LODGING

Your engagement is one of the busiest times of your life, and you often don't know whether you're coming or going. Well, now it's time to decide exactly *how* you'll be coming and going during your wedding festivities. You need to plan your grand entrance and exit as husband and wife. If you have several events planned for a weekend wedding, such as a rehearsal dinner and a post-wedding brunch, you have to figure out how your wedding party and out-of-town guests will get from place to place.

Whether you ride on a Harley or a horse, someone has to make the arrangements. Maybe Dad rented limos for your first wedding. As you do your "ride" research, you may look into more unique modes of transportation. Now that your tastes are more sophisticated, it probably isn't such a novelty to get the whole gang into a limo and cruise around the town drinking champagne and smoking cigars.

Your friends may know better than to camouflage the car with decorations and graffiti-like "just married" signs spray-painted all over your vehicle. You may not want crepe paper, balloons, or cans trailing from your bumper. You still can have decorations—you just may want the Bentley or Benz bedecked in style. Something simple and elegant. One couple chose to tie two small wildflower bouquets to the end of a rustic wooden "just married" sign before they drove away from their beautiful country wedding.

Perhaps you want to rent a Porsche or a Jaguar for the day. You can live out that fantasy, but you should be realistic about others. One bride wanted to descend to her reception from a helicopter with pink feathers falling from the sky. Her buttoned-up groom didn't exactly go for the idea.

Remember, second-time brides are more willing to break the rules and go against tradition. Think about your personal style and the type of vehicle that suits both you and your fiancé. You also want to consider your dress. If you have a big gown, you may be limited in your choice of vehicles. It may be tough to squeeze into a cab or a small sports car. If you rent a fabulous convertible, say so long to your intricate up-do. Maybe you should save the top-down drive for the end of the wedding instead of for the jaunt from the ceremony to the reception.

How many people will be riding with you? After the ceremony, do you want your children to ride in the horse-drawn carriage with you? Perhaps you will want to hire a few carriages for the day, and your children can ride behind you.

The yellow pages are a good resource. My husband needed to rent a bus for our out-of-town guests, and he found a company in the yellow pages. We didn't plan anything extravagant for our ride. My husband's best friend was nice enough to drive me to the hotel

Second-Time Smarts

Have a backup plan in place in case your hired ride is a no-show. It's a good idea to ask a friend to be "on call" to give you or your guests a ride to the wedding.

for my wedding. I was getting ready at the hotel so it wasn't a dramatic entrance. I was just in jeans, no makeup, carrying my bags.

You don't have to sign on for the typical limo ride. Don't be afraid to think outside the stretchmobile and have some fun. If you're planning a creative wedding, from the invitations to your attire, why not carry the theme over to your transportation? For example, if you are getting married at a mountain lodge, ski down the slope together. If you are having a campsite wedding, how about paddling away in a canoe to your own private beach across the lake? If you work for the fire department, perhaps you can arrange to drive off in a fire truck. One couple was recently featured in a magazine taking off into the fields on a tractor, she in her dress and he in his tux.

Your Getaway Ride

Many couples see their wedding as a time to splurge and do something special. Figure out how much of a statement you'd like to make in your entrance and exit. Do you want to be creative and leave the wedding in a hot-air balloon? Do you want to spend as little as possible on the rides? Do you have a great deal of coordinating to think about if your reception and ceremony are at different places and your out-of-town guests are staying at a third location and your rehearsal dinner is at a fourth? For some it may make sense to rent a luxury bus or trolley car. One couple had a trolley car take the guests from the hotel to the rehearsal dinner in downtown Minneapolis. It was fun, and it's great not worrying about figuring out directions in a strange city.

Of course, you may not have to splurge at all. Perhaps you own a vintage car or can borrow a friend's classic car or boat for your wedding. If you borrow a vehicle, make sure you or someone else cleans it and fills it up with gas before you return it.

If you want a horse-drawn carriage for the romance and amazing photo opportunities, go for it, but know it could take an hour to ride just a few miles. You may want to trot away in the carriage (get some great pictures) and then have a car or limo pick you up a block or so out of view. The carriages are *not* heated, but many companies offer blankets so you can have your picturesque winter wedding ride. Find out if you can see the carriage before your wedding to make sure it is in excellent condition. You'll also want to know how many horses are included, and whether or not two horses cost extra.

Questions to Ask Transportation Companies Before Signing On

- Do you charge by the hour or by the day?

- Do you charge by distance?

- Is there an overtime charge?

- When do you start charging—upon pickup or when the car leaves the garage?

- Are tolls and parking charges included?

- Is there a minimum period of time required?

- Are taxes included?

- Are tips included?

- What do you require for a deposit?

- When do you need the deposit?

- How many other events do you have on our wedding date?

- What is your cancellation policy?

- Can we see the vehicle before our wedding?

- Will there be a driver?

- What will the driver be wearing?

You shouldn't have to call a transportation company too far in advance, unless of course it's the height of prom season and your wedding is two weeks away. If that's the case, finding a limo will be a challenge. When you call, ask if the company has any wedding packages. They may give you a special rate and offer some extras like a "just got hitched" sign, champagne, and a chauffeur who will roll out a red carpet.

Think about how much renting you want to do. Do you need a ride to the airport? Do your guests need rides to and from the airport? Are you planning to accommodate everyone, or does your budget allow for only you and your groom? It helps to know how many people you need to transport up front, because the company may be able to give you a discount for renting several cars. Don't think only of out-of-towners. Perhaps you should plan for your grandmother to have a ride back to her home so she can leave when she gets tired and none of your other family members need to leave the party early.

Second-Time Smarts

Two limos can be cheaper than one! Instead of having the limo that took you from your ceremony site to your reception wait outside for hours, hire another one just to take you home. That way you don't have to pay the first limo to just sit there until you need it.

Other Details

• Make sure the contract lists all the stops you want the driver to make in your vehicle of choice.

• Make sure the company is licensed and insured.

• Make sure the driver and your contact at the transportation company have exact directions and contact information for your wedding coordinator, you, and the reception site.

• If your car is taking you only from the ceremony to the reception, don't forget to line up a ride home or back to your hotel. You don't want to have to hitch a ride in your wedding gown.

Why Not Valet?

Your guests will appreciate door-to-door service if you offer valet. No one wants to trudge through a parking lot of puddles or snow on their way to your reception. It's nice for clothes to remain dry and hair to remain in place. If your wedding is at a facility or out-door area that doesn't have on-site valet services, ask friends, family, and colleagues to refer you to a reputable company.

The Rooms

Where will your wedding party and out-of-town guests stay? And how about the close friends and family who choose not to drive home from a wedding that will end late? It's more fun for everyone to have them stay, and if they are drinking, it's safer.

It's a good idea to offer your out-of-town guests a few places to stay. I went to a wedding where guests had a choice of staying at two hotels or at cabins at the wedding ceremony site, depending on their preference for a rustic setting or maid service.

Call early to book the rooms and let your contact at the hotel know you'd like to reserve a block of rooms for your guests. The hotel should give your guests a special discounted group rate because they are part of your wedding. Make sure this is the best place for your out-of-town guests before handing over your credit card number to a hotel or inn. Think about proximity to the wedding and reception. Sure, the hotel lobby and spa rival any hot spot from South Beach to SoHo, but if it will take two hours in traffic for everyone to get to the rehearsal and ceremony, think again. You want your guests to arrive in a *good* mood. You also want to make sure you can get the nicest rooms for the best rate. Ideally, you want your guests to stay close to your city's main attractions so they can make a nice minivacation out of your wedding weekend.

Just the Two of You

Remember that you don't have to stay where your guests are staying. You may want to keep your location secret on your wedding night if you truly want to be alone and not have any guests knocking on your door.

Do you want a bed and breakfast? A hotel? Regardless of where you stay, make it clear when you book that it is your wedding night. You should be given some type of wedding suite or at least one of the best rooms. There also may be little extras included for the wedding.

16

Wait a Minute Mr. Postman

THE INVITATIONS

You've entertained on various occasions and know how to order invitations, but you may want to explore how wedding invitations are changing. Brides and grooms now take advantage of the plethora of papers available on the Internet, at stationery shops, crafts stores, and office-supply stores, and many use creative shapes, colors, and illustrations on their wedding invitations. Anything goes.

I browsed through many specialty stores and loved what I saw, from gorgeous red, hefty paper stock with gold beveled edges to delicate paper that has literally been rained on to look like colored lace. Elegance goes beyond black engraved lettering on white paper. You can create elegant invitations with colored ink or paper or with neutral hues. A simple embossed stamp design can go a long way.

Add a twist to the package and you can really wow your guests. Paper that appears aged or pressed with flowers can make lovely invitations rolled scroll-style and mailed in a tube. You can use satin ribbons, vellum overlays, or toggle-back envelopes. One bride sent her invitations in a clear plastic container. The actual invitation was wrapped in faux fur and tied with a bow.

You do not need to do something wild because you're a second-time bride, however. You can be as traditional as you want. If you want a formal white invitation engraved with black script in standard rectangular form, nothing is stopping you.

Watch the Bottom Line

Invitation costs can add up. In addition to the price of the paper, which varies according to quality, you have to consider the cost for printing method; amount of printing (it costs more to have your return address printed on the envelopes); embellishments (ribbons, photos, beads, dried flowers); the amount of materials you're sending; and postage. Whatever you choose, just be sure to order extra invitations for mistakes and keepsakes.

Second-Time Smarts

Instead of scribbling your own map, you can have one printed up professionally at Sigma Custom Wedding Maps (www.sigmamaps.com).

Printing

Printing methods vary from offset printing to the traditional and expensive engraving. A look that's similar to engraving—but less pricey—is thermography. The main difference is that the paper isn't indented. Some brides choose letterpress printing, an old-fashioned craft in which special plates are made. Julie Holcomb Printers (www.julieholcombprinters.com) is well known for letterpress invitations.

Postage

Wedding invitations can be quite the layered packet of papers. Some include an outer envelope, inner envelope, tissue paper divider, invitation, reception card, response card, self-addressed stamped envelope, and map with ceremony and reception directions.

Postal Refresher Course

• Take an invitation to the post office and have it weighed so you buy the right postage. You can peruse your stamp options at www.usps.com.

• Postage rates are usually higher for nonstandard-sized envelopes.

• If you make your own invitations, do a test mailing by sending one to yourself to see how it holds up in the mail.

• Ask the postmaster to hand-cancel them so they arrive in good condition.

• Mail invitations six to eight weeks before your wedding (no later than eight weeks for out-of-town invitations).

• You can save money by cutting out the invitation inserts. Putting everything on one page saves on printing and postage. You also help the environment. Many earth-conscious brides aren't interested in wasting paper with an envelope inside an envelope.

Keep It Personal

If you're trying to achieve elegance, don't even think about sending an e-mail invitation.

You can send informal invitations, but to just send out a mass e-mail looks like you didn't care enough to mail an invitation. Also, guests shouldn't e-mail that they are coming. They should take time to fill out the response card.

Use Technology

Today you can design beautiful invitations on your computer. Invitations you create are more personalized, and the process is probably less frustrating for you than looking through huge books of sample invitations. If you're not artistic, but still want a personalized invitation, you can hire an artist or graphic designer to create something just for you.

People usually can't tell the difference between calligraphy that's been done by hand and that done by computer. Having the envelopes addressed in elegant script by computer will save you a lot of money.

NORA'S STORY

I made my invitations using materials I bought at a paper wholesaler. I bought blank, ivory invitations with a "step up" border and matching envelopes. I pasted hand-made paper with a subtle stripe pattern over the center of the invitations and covered them with translucent ivory vellum, onto which I printed our names and date and a piece of clip art I'd found of a Jazz Age couple dancing. I used a star-shaped hole punch and threaded the cards with iridescent ribbon. The text was printed on the inside.

What to Say and How to Say It

Remember, you can word your invitations however you want. You can include a song or poem, a note to one another, a design or photo of something special to you both, or you can just have fun and include playful wording. The only rule that still applies is that the people paying get top billing. If your parents or his are paying, their names come first on the invitation. Even if you and your fiancé are paying for the wedding, you may still have your invitations issued with your parents' names, in order to honor them, or you can ignore tradition and not mention the parents at all.

If you want to include all the parents (regardless of who is paying) in order to please everyone, traditionally the bride's parents' names are printed first, followed by the groom's parents. It's up to you. This is *your* wedding.

Here's a peek at how some real brides' second-wedding invitations read.

Couple #1

This invitation was presented on recycled paper with pressed grass. The bride made the invitations herself on her computer and felt the informal approach was a good fit. She didn't want to tie the invitations with the usual bow so she collected more than 300 twigs outside in the middle of a Midwest winter to attach to the invitations.

"This day I will marry my best friend. The one I laugh with,
live for, dream with, love."
Mabel and Martin
Together with their parents
[bride's mom's name here]*
[bride's dad's name here]
[groom's mom's name here]
[groom's dad's name here]
Invite you to join them in celebrating their marriage on
Saturday, April 27, 2003, at half past six o'clock
[hotel name here]
[city, state here]
Reception to follow.

* Parents are divorced so they are listed separately.

Letting Your Kids in on the Invitations

• Ask your children to draw a picture for your invitations. Base your design on their colorful Crayola creation.

• How about a picture of you, your fiancé, and your children on the invitation, with your kids inviting the guests?

• A great way to include your kids and make them feel special is to put their names on the invitation:

Mabel
With her daughter, Frannie
and her son, Tommy
and
Martin
With his son, John
Request the pleasure of your company
At the union of their families

Couple #2

Once upon a time there lived a lonely Diva,
Mabel
One day her fairy godmother appeared and
granted Diva a magical wish. Diva wished
to live happily ever after with her Prince Charming,
Martin
You are invited to take part in this magical union.
Friday, July 21, 2003

At 5:00 in the evening
[address here]
[city, state here]
Reception immediately following the Diva's Wish.

Couple #3

Though the wedding was formal, parts of the invitation were printed in white lettering with hot pink, yellow, and orange in the background. You don't have to follow the rules and issue an ecru-colored, heavy stock invitation with English Script in order to send the message that your wedding is formal. Couple #3 let people know how to dress on the bottom of the invitation: "Black tie and tiaras."

The invitation was an incredibly creative package with several parts to it. Here is the wording in one section to give you an idea of how the bride and groom let their personal flair shine:

Wedding Day Reflections

If there was anything I'd do differently about my wedding it would be the invitations. We made the invitations ourselves, which was stressful. The paper we picked to make our envelopes was so fibrous it wouldn't hold a stamp. We ended up having to make envelopes for the envelopes!

—Jim

When you have the challenge of planning a wedding for a gray suit and his cheetah print obsessed bride . . . what do you do?
You give them both what they want.
Since he's the yin to her yang, she's the salt to his pepper, he's the metal to her magnet, and she's the sugar to his lemon drop, you're receiving invitations to "two" events. His and hers.
On [date here], pin stripes meet leopard spots to celebrate the merger of Mabel and Martin.

If you want a traditional invitation, you are by all means entitled. I just thought I'd show you some examples of invitations you may not come across while researching different styles in magazines, books, and on the Web. Invitation articles always say it's important that your invitation make the first impression and cue guests in on what to expect for the festivities and how to dress. I say create and send out the invitation you want. Don't try to limit yourself with rules. Your friends and families can ask you how to dress, or you can list the formality on the invitation, such as "Black tie" or "Bare feet welcome."

Ways to Word

The scenarios and wording for invitations are practically endless. Nonrelatives may host and invite guests to your wedding; both sets of parents may host; or you and your groom may host the wedding but still want to include your deceased parents' names. If you have any questions about your situation, ask your invitation specialist or wedding coordinator for assistance.

If you and your groom are paying for the wedding, here are two ways your invitation can read:

The honour of your presence is requested
at the marriage of
Mabel
to
Martin

(or)

Mabel
and
Martin
request the honour of your presence
at their marriage.

If you are inviting guests to the reception only:

The pleasure of your company
is requested
at the wedding reception of
Mabel
and
Martin
Saturday, the twenty-eighth of September
at
seven o'clock in the evening
[address here]
[city, state here]
Black tie

Los Angeles wedding coordinator Mindy Weiss says second-time brides are keeping their invitations simple and traditional. "Usually the first time around they learned from their mistakes and now they want to keep it simple," she says. "The wording will usually come from the bride and groom, but I also have parents who do both weddings."

Mindy offers two options for wording second-wedding invitations:

Mabel
and
Martin
request the pleasure of your company
at their marriage
[date here]
[year here]
[time here]
[place here]

(or)

Please join us at our
Marriage Ceremony and Celebration
[date here]
[year here]
[time here]
[place here]
Mabel and Martin

17

The Creative Touch

WRITING VOWS AND TOASTS, AND PRESERVING A PIECE OF YOUR DAY

You chose the ceremony you want, and you can choose the words that will connect you as husband and wife. Your vows may be the most significant words you ever say to one another, so you may want to have a hand in what they convey.

Writing Your Own Vows

Many couples don't want to repeat the same vows they spoke at their first weddings, but they're not sure what to write or how to get started. Even if you don't consider yourself the least bit poetic, you can still scribe some beautiful words to recite at your wedding. They don't have to be religious or formal. They can be all about your relationship or your feelings. You may want to share with your loved ones how grateful you are now or talk about the person you are today and how far you've come. You can express your excitement about the journey ahead, or you can read a love letter. You don't have to speak in phrases such as, "I promise . . ." You can speak freely. Perhaps you want to recite words from your favorite children's story or song. You can look through your journal, old pictures, or scrapbooks for inspiration, or think back to when you first fell in love or got engaged.

Your vows don't have to be long; they just have to be from your heart. Make sure you show each other what you plan to say and to practice together before the big day. Here are some original vows from real second-time couples.

Couple #1

I, [name here], take you, [name here], to be my partner in marriage and in life. I promise to love you and honor you, to be faithful to you, to stand by you in good times and in bad, to fill your life with happiness and laughter, to show you respect, and to be your wife/husband and companion until death do us part.

Couple #2

His: "[Name here], there are so many things that I love so much about you. It would be impossible to talk about them all today. But there's one thing about you that I do want to talk about, and that's your smile. It's what brought me to you and it's what keeps us strong. There's nothing else you can say or do that sends a stronger message that you love me, that you love being with me. It truly brightens my day and my life. Today, [Name here], in front of everybody here that I love, I promise to you forever to try to make you smile. I love you."

Hers: "I have fallen hopelessly and undeniably in love with you. Since you have been in my life, I have felt an unbelievable sense of completion. I never thought I could love someone as much as I love you. And with every moment that passes, my love for you grows stronger and deeper. You are my soul mate. I recently heard someone define a soul mate as 'the person who makes you the most you could ever possibly be.' You bring out the best in me. Thank you for loving me the way that you do and for always keeping me laughing and smiling. [Name here], I promise to be your best friend, to respect you and support you, to work together as a team to achieve our goals, to love you more and more each day, and when you fall I will catch you; when you cry I will comfort you; and when you laugh I will share in your joy. I will forever love you."

Wedding Newsletters and Your Own Wedding Web Site

Maybe for your first wedding you mailed out-of-towner letters with the pertinent details, including everything from hotel information to times of the wedding weekend festivities. Today you can do more than just inform—you can entertain. Send out a wedding newsletter or, better yet, create a wedding Web site. Throughout your engagement, friends and families can check in to see recent photos of you, find out about the hotel where they'll be staying, maybe peruse the menu for the rehearsal dinner, and read updates about how you and your fiancé are doing. This is especially great for out-of-towners who haven't seen you in a while and who haven't yet met your groom.

Your Web site can show pictures of your reception site, offer weather forecasts, introduce your wedding party, and share the story of how you got engaged (it will save lots of long-distance calls). The site allows you to remain in contact with your family and friends throughout your engagement. It's also fun for posting pictures of your wedding after you get back from your honeymoon.

Writing Toasts

I know about writing speeches and toasts. My mom—Susan Weingarden, owner of Portraits in Poetry—gets paid to write them for everyone else. She can put peoples' thoughts and emotions into words, and will even do it in rhyme. I asked her to share some tips on writing wedding speeches and toasts. Susan says you can add humor, but always use good taste—never embarrass or hurt anyone.

If you are wondering how to get started on writing a speech or toast to your groom, Susan suggests starting with small sections. Here are some sample topics:

- Welcome everyone.
- Share a bit of your history or tell about how you met.
- Share some of your husband's personality traits, outstanding qualities, and hang-ups.
- Talk about how you are different and also how you are alike.
- Mention things you both like, things you do together, and things you disagree about.
- Explain what you love about him and what he means to you.
- Compliment his family.
- End with good wishes for your future.

Wedding Day Reflections

All of our guests were out of town. We did a Web site and a letter with lots of information about different hotels they can stay at and included some travel Web sites for airline tickets. We also included a schedule of events for the weekend and a list of things to do, like golf or hitting the spa.

—Jessica

Toasting Taboos

- Getting drunk.
- Referencing your first wedding or first husband.

- Sharing inside jokes or raunchy humor.
- Snubbing family members (can't mention one child and not the other).
- Speaking too softly or quickly.
- Talking, and talking, and talking . . .

Programs

Ceremony programs are a great opportunity to let your creativity show. Your guests can enjoy a unique booklet of your own design while they learn about the order of your ceremony and the readings and songs you've chosen. Designing your own program also allows you to include a little description of each person who is in your wedding party, honor deceased loved ones with a special message, thank guests for coming, and even explain various religious rituals that will be performed in your ceremony.

One bride created a six-page program correlating with her unique fairy-tale theme. It listed the evening's activities, including:

Presentation of Diva and Prince
    Charming
Introductions of Diva's Divine Wedding Party
Jumping the Broom Ceremony
Champagne Toast of Enchanted Wishes
The Garter, In Search of the Next Prince

Wedding Day Reflections

I made programs using ivory card stock with an overlay of spring green vellum, tied with gold tassels. I preserved the stephanotis that I didn't use in the floral arrangements and included it as part of the design for my scrapbook pages. We also have a Web site my husband created.

—Nora

Creative Place Cards

Place cards don't have to be cards. In fact, they don't have to come close to resembling paper or a small rectangular shape at all. You can paint table numbers on flowerpots, pumpkins, leaves, or picture frames. They can tie into your theme or color scheme. Are you having an outdoor wedding by the water? How about displaying a table of smooth rocks painted with your guests' names and table numbers at the reception area's entrance? Are you having a sushi blowout? Try tying place cards to pairs of chopsticks.

For decorative tools, try Michaels (www.michaels.com) or www.scrapbookingwithus.com. See the Resources section for other crafts and keepsake companies.

Stocking the Out-of-Towner Goodie Bag

After a harried trip of traveling and finally checking into the hotel, it's nice to get to your room and catch a glance of a welcome bag, courtesy of the bride and groom. Don't be surprised if famished guests dig in and tear open the bag of chips or trail mix before they even read your welcome letter or schedule of events for the weekend. Some couples offer a map of the area, scented candles, a list of activities, bottled water, snacks, fruit, and mints. You can play up your hometown flavor or the destination of your wedding. For example, here in Michigan, a bride could include Michigan dried cherries, maple syrup, honey, and jam.

Loading up the out-of-towner bags can be a fun project for the kids. Even if you don't have kids yourself, you can recruit your nieces and nephews or neighbors. Just offer a reward of some treats to take home with them. Your mom and possibly your sister may want to help, but other than that, it's pretty much up to you and your guy. You don't want to put your friends to work. It probably won't take you that long anyway. Try to find a bulk food store or warehouse so you can buy items such as bottled water, trail mix, candy, granola bars, pretzels, and chips at a discount. The hotel can give the bags to your guests when they check in, but it's up to you to drop off the bags at the hotel ahead of time.

Wedding Keepsakes

When the party is over, you have your photos and your memories. But some brides want to create something special with their wedding memorabilia. Beautiful keepsakes will help jog those wedding memories, and they're wonderful treasures for future generations. An ornate frame or decorated box with special items from your wedding day inside is one more way to savor the day you truly became one.

Perhaps you were too busy to even consider researching such memory-making projects before your first wedding. I know I was. I was overwhelmed with the task of selecting "stuff," from tablecloths to teacups. And to be honest, I had no idea how many resources are available to help preserve wedding treasures.

My Creative Keepsakes

I'm sentimental. I'll save anything. I saved all the movie stubs from the first two years of dates with my husband. I can't throw away photographs even if I have three copies of the same one. My grandmothers both know that any item with a history will find a home with me. My future grandchildren may not be savers, or even sentimental for that matter, but if they are, I'll have several keepsakes to hand down. I had our wedding invitation professionally framed, and I sealed a special box of memorabilia from our wedding day. I plan to mount the items into a shadow box frame of some sort. The box contains the wedding vows we wrote, our seating card, a cocktail napkin with our initials and wedding date, the garter I wore (which my mother wore when she married my father), and dried flowers from my bouquet. We also received some special gifts that are beautiful keepsakes. My cousins bought us a beautiful artistic ketubah (Jewish marriage contract), and a couple of our dear friends had the glass Bobby stepped on during our ceremony made into a beautiful mezuzah.

Making Magical Memories

You can save what you wore and carried down the aisle, or you can go a step further and preserve them. Take your wedding gown to a dry cleaner and have it preserved in an archival box, wrapped in acid-free tissue.

You can make your gown into a bridal bed quilt or turn it into christening gowns for your future children. You can have photos from your wedding copied onto fabric to make into a quilt.

Hurry your bouquet to a floral preservationist so your blooms can be freeze-dried to look the way they did on your wedding day. (You can contact the International Freeze-Dry Floral Association at 888-554-0907 or www.ifdfa.com.)

Air dry your flowers and display them in a frame or save them in a keepsake box. You can have the pressed petals made into candles. Your flowers can also be laminated into a bookmark or applied to ceramic tiles you can hang in your home or build into your kitchen or bathroom. You can make a three-dimensional shadow box collage of your wedding keepsakes, such as your husband's boutonniere and a photo of your first dance. Your invitation or vows can be engraved onto special heirloom pieces of silver.

You may even come up with your own ideas for things that haven't been done before. Many of these projects can wait until after your honeymoon, of course, but at least remember to save pieces of your day!

Getting Gorgeous

ACCESSORIES, HAIR, AND MAKEUP

The beauty of this not being your first wedding is that you have your own money to spend at the salon. You don't need Mom's permission or checkbook to get your hair put up in a fury of loops on top of your head.

Treat yourself to those little salon and spa perks that will make you feel even more beautiful on your wedding day. If you want to touch up your hair color or get a peel, go ahead, but don't do anything drastic. It's not a good idea to get major plastic surgery or change your hair from brown to platinum blonde before your wedding. After all, you want your guests (and your groom) to recognize you.

Accessorize This

Your accessory options range from hairpins to hankies, and they are as practical as they are pretty. A beautiful lace handkerchief would make a special keepsake to pass down to your daughter one day, and you will need to wipe your tears on something other than your husband's sleeve anyway. Remember, every piece of your outfit will be in pictures. Will you wear a cape or a wrap? A little mink stole or luxurious pashmina shawl? You have many options, from embroidered cardigans to Spanish-style shawls to your husband's jacket.

Your gown is undoubtedly fabulous. Now you get to think about how you want to accent it. For advice on bridal accessories, I turned to one of the top experts in the industry, Tammy Darling (www.tammydarling.com). Tammy's designs, including bridal bags, combs, tiaras, and veils, have been featured in *In Style* magazine. "A bride can have a great dress and fall short of pulling together her look because she purchases the wrong accessories," she says. Fortunately, a little guidance is all you may need.

Accessory options have changed since your first wedding. "The greatest thing about bridal accessories today is that the headpieces are more like hair ornaments or hair jewelry," Tammy says. "Whether a tiara, comb, or pins, you can make the accessory work with your hair and you don't have to fit your hair to the accessory."

You can also accessorize with flowers. Wear a floral wreath in your hair or accent your hair with flowers. Wear your long hair down and wavy, with just one flower tucked behind your ear.

Here's what you need to know when shopping for headwear:

1. **How do you want to wear your hair?** What style looks best on you? What will look best with your dress? For example, you can show off your beautiful neck and collarbones when you wear your hair up with a strapless gown.

2. **What is your gown like?** What color is it? What is the style? How is it embellished? Are there pearls or crystals? If so, are they clear or iridescent?

3. **Take a day or two—outside of shopping for your gown—to look at headpieces.** Try on different styles. You can clip

out pictures from magazines or bring pictures you found on the Internet. Never let the bridal salon pressure you into purchasing a headpiece when you buy the gown. Some salespeople will tell you the headpiece won't match the gown if you don't buy it together. In reality, bridal salons often have limited accessories, Tammy says.

4. **Some headwear looks great with certain hairstyles.** If you wear a low updo, think hairpins; for a blunt cut, try wearing a tiara as a headband. If your hair is really short, try a small beaded comb.

Professionally Speaking

I wish I had a makeup artist. I spent all that money on my wedding and had a shiny face and it showed up in pictures. It's worth having an expert making sure your hair looks great and that your hair will hold up.

—Beth Reed Ramirez,
editor of *Bride Again*

If you want to wear a veil, you can. A veil can look exceptionally good with a simple dress like a sheath. "A single-layer chapel or cathedral-length veil can look exquisite," says Tammy. "I love showing a bride how she can drape the long veil over her arm with her bouquet."

Some places to browse or shop online:

www.tammydarling.com
www.homabridal.com
www.heavenlyheadpieces.com
www.wintersandrain.com

Ditching the Diet Efforts

There is a difference in pampering yourself pre-wedding this time around. You know not to starve yourself for five months before the big day. You don't want to end up walking down the aisle looking like a bony chicken. Besides, the weight comes right back on when you start eating again (which begins immediately on the honeymoon), and then you always have to look back at your wedding pictures and say, "Oh, I'll never be as thin as I was on my wedding day." Why pressure yourself to get stick-thin? You picked a dress that looks sensational on your body as it is, not your body minus 20 pounds. Remember, if you drop weight your gown will fit differently, and sometimes extreme alterations will ruin the original look of your gown.

Hair

Stylists recommend not having your hair colored or cut at the last minute. It's a good idea to get color or highlights and a trim about two weeks before your big day. If you're getting an updo, don't wash your hair the day of your wedding—wash it the day before. It will be easier for the stylist to shape and pin your hair if it is a little oily. Updos are always elegant, and the bonus is you don't have to play with your hair throughout the night. You can ask your stylist about a French knot, chignon, bun, or braid. But if you wear your hair up, try to avoid the urge to have your stylist leave straight or curled strands at the sides of your face. By the end of the night they'll end up frizzed and scraggly. And don't wear too much hairspray. You don't want to look too stiff.

If you plan on wearing flowers in your hair, you need to have a trial run. Order the flowers from your florist, who will attach them to wires so your stylist can securely pin them in your hair.

Face

Makeup is a must, but before we begin, let's focus on skin. Achieving the perfect glow has as much to do with what's underneath as it does with what's on top. "Your face is a focal point on your wedding day, and healthy, well-nourished skin is the canvas," says Tamra Auzenne, a cosmetic artist and esthetician at Therapeutic Esthetics in South Pasadena, California. Tamra recommends monthly facials rich in vitamins and minerals, such as the oxygen facial many celebrities choose. It helps to repair free-radical damage and build healthy collagen in the skin, she says. She also suggests using customized home skin-care products that contain botanicals and seaweed elements.

If facials aren't in your budget, you can still follow my tips: drink lots of water, get at least eight hours of sleep, exfoliate, and wear moisturizer with sunscreen.

Now for makeup. Experts agree that no matter how natural you like to appear, you should not go bare-faced on your wedding day. "There isn't a bride out there who couldn't benefit from wearing makeup on her wedding day," says Todd Skog, owner of Todd's Room in Birmingham, Michigan, a hair and makeup salon that specializes in bridal beauty. Todd, a nationally accredited makeup artist who has worked with actress Cybill Shepherd and has done the makeup for the covers of *Allure* and *Jet* magazines, says that second-time brides have usually learned what *not* to do with their hair and makeup.

Todd recommends oil-free and waterproof makeup and a soft matte finish. They are best for photos. If you use makeup with a shiny finish or a glimmer, the light tends to bounce back into the camera and cause red-eye. You also don't want your face to look shiny in the pictures.

Professionally Speaking

Celebrities are allowed to be as decadent as they want, no matter how many times they marry. Brides see that they shouldn't feel ashamed that it's their second time getting married and that they can be as beautiful as they want.

—Tammy Darling,
accessories designer

More Tips from Todd

On bridal blunders: The biggest mistakes I see are brides wearing too much makeup, too little makeup, and doing their own makeup.

On quick fixes for looking young: If you've already done Botox or had peels, go ahead, but if you've never had any of these treatments done, don't chance it because you never know how your skin is going to react.

On eyebrow arches: It's extremely important that an arch is done properly so it flatters your face. If it's not done right, it can ruin your look. The right arch can make you look like you had an instant face-lift. It opens the eyes and brings out the cheekbones.

On lips: If you want your lipstick to stay on all night, wear a matte finish lipstick, lip gloss, and a lipstick sealer. Red lipstick looks good on everyone so long as you find the right shade, a good liner, and put them on properly.

On touch-ups: You need to bring certain beauty items with you to your wedding for touch-ups: pressed powder, oil blotting papers, blush, lip liner, and lipstick or gloss.

Before you book the makeup artist and hairstylist for your wedding, schedule a test appointment. Bring in a photo or magazine picture of how you'd like your hair to look. You are essentially testing the beauty experts to make sure they will do what you want. You don't want any surprises on your wedding day.

It's worth every penny to have professionals do your hair and makeup and have them travel to your location. You don't want to be stuck leaving the salon in a rainstorm. Whether you are getting married in a hotel, a church, or at home, hire the stylists to come to the room where you will get ready. This way you don't have to worry about the elements ruining your hair or makeup.

Many brides get ready with a swarm of bridesmaids around them. If you were one of those brides at your first wedding, how did that work for you? I've talked to many women who say it was stressful having 10 bridesmaids fixing their hair and dresses and chattering and giving a countdown of how many hours and minutes until the wedding. You might want to consider getting ready alone or in a room with just immediate family—your daughter, sister, or mother. My mother and I got ready in a hotel suite the afternoon of my wedding and we ordered room service for lunch. It was nice to just have some quiet time to myself and then surprise my bridesmaids later when I was all dressed and glammed up in my gown.

Shoes

Sexy shoes are the rage and you don't have to settle for less on your wedding day, whether you want a fabulous Jimmy Choo ankle-strap with sequins or a lace open-toe mule by Manolo Blahnik. If your dress is simple, you can draw more attention to your shoes. I've seen little mules with wedge heels, slingbacks with rhinestones, and sandals with crystals. You can stick with a low satin pump or an ankle-strap stiletto. It's up to you. Many clothing designers are offering bridal shoes now, including Ralph Lauren, Cynthia Rowley, Calvin Klein, and Richard Tyler.

No matter how fabulouso the shoes, you are not going to be a happy bride if you can't walk in them. Select shoes that are comfortable for walking, dancing, and standing all night. You may want to wear heels for the ceremony and then switch to ballet slippers or flats for the reception.

If you are wearing a long gown, you don't have to purchase beautiful beaded or satin shoes, because no one will see them. Instead, go for comfort. You can wear ballet slippers or tennis shoes instead of tottering on heels all night, and you also won't tower over your groom. If you plan on buying new shoes, don't get hung up on the size. The best thing to do is to try on shoes at the end of the day when your feet are more swollen. Be sure you scuff up the soles of the shoes before your wedding. You don't want to fall on your face in the foyer. If you want to dye your shoes to match your dress, bring a swatch of your dress fabric.

Want to check out shoes online? Try:

www.myglassslipper.com
www.stuartweitzman.com
www.kennethcole.com
www.bridalshoes.com
www.designershoes.com

Beauty Schedule

Don't get everything done the day of your wedding. You'll be exhausted (not to mention possibly red and bumpy) before you even show up for pictures. Here's a beauty time sheet:

Hair color and cut: 2 weeks before

Waxing (legs, lip, bikini . . .): 1 week before

Facial: 3 weeks before

Manicure: 1 day before

Pedicure: 1 week to 1 day before

Eyebrow arch: 2 days before

Makeup: Wedding day

Massage: Anytime before your wedding except your wedding day. Your muscles may feel like Jell-O, and you don't want to be so relaxed you can't even walk down the aisle.

Jewelry

You may not have given much thought to jewelry when it came time for your first wedding. Your mom probably said "pearls" and you went with pearls. This time you can do anything you want with jewelry, whether costume or real. Just keep it simple and elegant. If your dress is elaborate, you need to keep your jewelry very simple, perhaps as little as a pair of earrings.

Be sure to put your jewels on last! You don't want the film and fog of your powder and hairspray to land on your sparkling stones.

Bridal Bouquet

It may just be the most recognizable accessory to date: the bridal bouquet. "Bridal bouquets for second-time brides are smaller scale because many of them are not wearing traditional wedding dresses," says Dale Morgan, co-owner of Blossoms in Birmingham, Michigan. "They are wearing glamorous Hollywood-style dresses that are a little more daring, and the bouquet is downplayed."

For something a little different, your florist can tie branches, vines, ivy, leaves, curly willow, long grasses, and sticks into your bouquet. Some brides want little crystals added to their flowers to match their earrings, or they like detailing on the handle such as pearls or crystal beads.

Bruce Bolton, owner of Breath of Spring in Bloomfield Hills, Michigan, says most brides choose simple hand-tied bouquets today. Carrying loose flowers in your arms is not very common. Stems wrapped in satin or ribbon and pinned

Professionally Speaking

This may not be your first wedding, but it's your *right* wedding.
—Bruce Bolton, owner of Breath of Spring

Second-Time Smarts

No matter how tired you are after the rehearsal dinner or how many drinks you had, don't go to bed with your makeup on. Wash your face even if it takes every ounce of energy you have left. You'll be thankful in the morning when you wake up blemish-free.

with a beautiful pendant or family heirloom is a beautiful look, Bruce says, and some brides have their bridal bouquet wrapped in fabric cut from their gown during alterations. It's a special way to tie your whole look together.

A Girl's Best Friends

CHOOSING ATTENDANTS

If you picture your wedding day with your nearest and dearest friends by your side but you're not sure if you should have bridesmaids, don't worry. You can have a bridal party, and it can be as large as you want. Though many second-time brides choose fewer attendants, and some tap their tots for the honorary roles, there are no restrictions. Don't let anyone tell you that you can't have your closest friends or family members in the wings when you exchange your vows. Surround yourselves with the people who are most meaningful to you.

You probably know from experience that in many respects it's actually a drag to stand up in a wedding. You have to get your hair and face done, be there early, and sit around in your dress for hours before the ceremony. It's expensive because you usually have to buy something to wear and also entertain for the bride, which often means buying a gift in addition to a wedding and shower gift.

Now let me tell you the real bottom line: Your close friends wouldn't miss being a part of your wedding for the world.

241

I had bridesmaids at my second wedding—not as many as I had at my first, but I still chose to have my dearest friends stand up for me when I married Bobby. I even had two matrons of honor! My only concern was making sure my bridesmaids didn't spend money on buying another bridesmaid's dress. I asked them to wear a black dress of their choice, and they were thrilled. They were happy to just pick something out of their closet and not have to look like a carbon copy of every other bridesmaid. The pictures look so cool because I'm wearing white, they're wearing black, and the flowers are rich jewel-toned colors that are gorgeous against their black dresses. Each bridesmaid added a little of her unique style to her attire. Two of them wore strapless tops with long black skirts, two wore tank-style dresses, and two wore wraps. It was a nice mix and they all liked that they blended in with the rest of the guests instead of gallivanting around the ballroom in matching taffeta dresses that screamed "bridesmaid."

Second-time brides choose to have fewer attendants for various reasons. Sometimes their friends have changed over the years. Maybe they feel they are burdening friends by asking them to "re–stand up." You know your friends well, and if you feel comfortable asking them to be your bridesmaids, go right ahead. Just don't pick your bridesmaids for the wrong reasons. If it was 10 years ago that you stood up for someone or if you are no longer friends, you don't have to ask them. Weddings are about celebrating your love with those closest to you now, not then.

If your groom is having eight guys stand up for him, and you were planning on having five friends, don't feel you have to rustle

---

Wedding Day Reflections

We didn't have a bridal party, even though it was my husband's first wedding. We just wanted everyone to have fun and not have any obligations attached to the evening in terms of mandatory dresses or picture-taking.

—Beth

up some more attendants just so you can have an even number. It doesn't matter. Have who you want and don't get hung up on the number or how an uneven number will look during the ceremony. You don't even have to have your wedding party stand up. They can walk down the aisle and then sit in the first row and watch the ceremony. Imagine that! When you are standing in a wedding you can never see what's going on. You are always staring at the back of some other bridesmaid's head. I once stood up in a wedding and had the honor of being one of four women to carry the chuppah (wedding canopy in Jewish ceremonies) down the aisle. After we brought it onto the temple's bimah, we sat down and watched the ceremony. We had the best seats in the house.

Not only is it okay for you to have bridesmaids, it's fine if you want to have brides*men*. Male attendants are absolutely acceptable. If your brother is your best friend, go ahead and ask him to stand up for you. He'll wear what the groomsmen are wearing, but he'll stand on your side. Of course, the coed rule goes both ways. Your groom can have his close female friends stand up for him.

For Me?

Single women across the land appreciate it when the bride personally hands her beautiful bouquet to one of her friends. Let's face it, no self-respecting woman older than 30 wants to jockey for a flying batch of posies. Presenting a friend with the bouquet is an elegant way to be singled out. I was handed the bouquet at a wedding after dating Bobby only six weeks. It was the wedding of one of his best friends, and I don't know how he and his bride knew what we didn't even know yet!

Unique Ways to Ask Them to Stand Up

In the spirit of creativity, why not ask your attendants to stand up in a unique way? My husband jumped all over this concept. He created his own mock subpoenas (yes, he's a lawyer) and sent them to our friends. Some of them were actually scared when they received a formal "legal" document, but when they saw what it was they got a kick out of it. According to the document, my bridesmaids were "required" to wear a black dress of their choice.

Attendants' Attire

Whether pregnant or plus-size, bony or busty, all of your friends can find an outfit they will enjoy wearing all night. If you decide to choose something for them to purchase, ask these questions:

- Can she dance in it?
- Can she sit and the dress not rip?
- Can she wear a bra under it?

There are so many options today that are classy and sophisticated (two terms not often associated with bridesmaids' dresses). There are sweater sets, long skirts with cashmere cardigans and camisoles, sheaths, and pantsuits. You can mix and match separates or colors. Many companies offer several different styles of tops and skirts in order to flatter different body shapes.

When Bridesmaids Complain

- Though your friends are dear to you, don't even think about bringing them with you to pick out their bridesmaids' dresses.

They'll each start lobbying for the color and style of their choice, and you'll be caught in a situation trying to find a dress that pleases everyone.

• Wondering how to deal with your friends who are not friends? Isn't it amazing how you can be so close to two people who can't stand each other? You shouldn't have to worry that they'll elbow each other off the altar during the ceremony. Talk to each of them alone before the wedding and ask them to put their feelings aside for one weekend.

• If your maids don't seem happy for you, brush it off. Is your little sister loathing that you are getting all the attention? Are your friends complaining about the packed schedule of events? Just remember it's not your job to help them deal with their issues. You've got a wedding to focus on.

Wedding Day Reflections

My three bridesmaids lived in different locations along the Eastern seaboard, so I deliberately ordered very simple dresses for them: purple chiffon layered over mid-calf purple satin sheaths. My bridesmaids sent me their measurements and the dress shop did the rest!

—Alexandra

In all fairness, don't give your bridesmaids a reason to complain. If you have nothing but bridal business on the brain, you'll become a bore. Remember that although this is your time, you may have to keep some thoughts private. Your friends are busy too, and they have other things going on besides your wedding.

She's Off Duty

The nicest thing you can do for your bridesmaids is to not give them any bridesmaids' duties. Don't ask them to put out fires, deal with the DJ, or baby-sit the flower girls. Let your mom relax too. Hire a wedding coordinator and let her worry about the supply of bobby pins or breath mints at your primping station.

What About Bachelorette Bashes?

Many second-time brides are saying "no thanks" to the traditional bachelorette bashes. What they crave is more downtime with the girls. They have hectic lives and feel they don't see their girlfriends as much as they used to, so quality time is key. Here are some popular choices:

- Dessert and wine at a friend's house.
- A small group dinner at your favorite restaurant.
- A shopping spree (making a day of it either to the mall, outlet stores, or downtown).
- A weekend retreat camping, biking, skiing, or hiking.
- A day at the spa.

Butterfly Keepers, Flower Girls, and Best Boys

LETTING YOUR KIDS JOIN IN

According to the Stepfamily Association of America, about 46 percent of all marriages involve at least one partner who has been married before. Sixty-five percent of remarriages involve children from a previous marriage. It's hardly a rarity for the children to participate.

Preparing Your Children for Your Marriage

Talk to your kids about what to expect. Let them know how many people will be at your wedding, who they will see there, what exactly happens at a wedding, and what they can expect to do. You want them to picture how the night will evolve. Let them know that some of their favorite foods and desserts will await them, and that they can stay up late and see their grandparents from out of town. It's never too early to start getting them excited. If they are in the wedding, you really want them to start practicing a few months before, so walking straight while carrying a pillow becomes almost second nature.

Involving Your Little Ones Throughout Your Engagement

Keep in mind that the happiest time in your life may not be such a joyous time for your children. They may not feel as attached to your fiancé as you do and they may be concerned you'll move on and leave them behind. Although your engagement is a most exciting time, try not to get so caught up in the planning that you're tuning out your children. Even if you have a pile of work to do at night and tons of bridal magazines to sift through, pay attention to what they are trying to tell you, whether it's about what they did in gym class today or how they feel about you getting remarried. They may have been initially excited when you announced your engagement, but getting a little sad as the day approaches. Be sure to reassure them that you love them. Emphasize that they hold an important place in your family, and that is never going to change.

Don't be surprised if your children experience conflicting emotions. They may want you to be happy but at the same time fear that their soon-to-be stepparent is a wedge between you and their father. They don't know what to expect from the wedding day and beyond. They may be angry and lash out with hurtful words, or they may

Professionally Speaking

Kids have different temperaments. Some may be excited to be in the wedding ceremony. But if your son hates your fiancé, don't force him to say vows or to be the best man. You can tell your kids you'd like them to be in the wedding, but let them choose. Kids need to freely express their feelings, and if they don't want to be involved that's okay.

—Beth Reed Ramirez, editor of *Bride Again*

be very quiet throughout your engagement and shrug their shoulders when you ask for their opinion on photos and flowers.

"Every step of the way your children should be part of the celebration," says Diane Forden, editor in chief of *Bridal Guide* magazine. "You want them to feel included. Your wedding might be frightening for them because it's a new beginning."

• Ask them to look through bridal magazines with you to help Mommy pick out a dress.

• Bring them along while you go dress shopping.

• Have them suggest some songs for the band or DJ to play.

• Ask them to help you pick out the invitations.

• Ask them to help you stuff invitations.

• Let them try the cake and give their opinions at the cake-tasting.

Possible Roles for Your Kids

There are many ways to include your children in the wedding itself. Two obvious roles are serving as flower girls or ringbearers, but you can actually give them duties that are traditionally "adult" roles. For example, your husband doesn't have to have a best man. His son—or your son—can be his "best boy." Your daughter can be a bridesmaid or your maid of honor. If you and your fiancé both have kids, they can make up your whole wedding party.

As mentioned in chapter 8, which covers ceremonies, you can also honor your children by asking them to give a special reading, sing a song, or play an instrument. Perhaps you'd like your daughter to play piano as you walk down the aisle. The children can read a poem or letter they wrote, or you can choose a reading together.

The more they feel a part of your day, the more they will feel special and look back on the day with fond memories.

With the growing number of second weddings, it's become more popular for couples to include their children in their vows. Dr. Roger Coleman, president of Clergy Services, Inc., wanted a way to include children in remarriage ceremonies, so he created what he calls a "Family Medallion." It is given to the children in a special ceremony as a symbol of the bride and groom's commitment to their new family. The medallions are available in pendants, rings, charm bracelets, and lapel pins. Dr. Coleman says 15,000 medallions are sold each year through wedding-related stores, chapels, and on the Internet at www.family medallion.com. After you are declared husband and wife, your children are invited to come forward and receive their medallion along with a pledge of love and support from their new parent. Dr. Coleman says this helps strengthen the bonds in stepfamilies.

Making vows to each other *and* your children can make a huge difference in your children's attitude toward your wedding. You want them to feel they are becoming part of a stronger family, not that they are losing their mother to someone else.

One bride I interviewed wanted to give her stepdaughter a special honor and asked her to lead the guests in a post-ceremony celebration during which 100 butterflies were released. (Many bridal magazines have

Wedding Day Reflections

I'm 27 and I just had a second wedding. It felt more like the beginning of a marriage and not a "show." My husband and I both had large weddings the first time around, and it was important to us to have an intimate and meaningful ceremony. I just remember the chaos surrounding the planning of my first wedding. This time I wanted to remember the meaning of my wedding. We decided to include my three-year-old daughter from my previous marriage in the ceremony. My husband presented her with her own little gold wedding band and a special vow he had written. She is *still* telling people *she* got married!

—Karen

ads from companies who offer butterfly celebrations for weddings.) Another ceremony idea is to have your family light a pillar candle made of several tapers, one for each person to light, so no one is left out.

You may also want to add a little surprise. Write a special note to your children in the wedding program so everyone can see how special they are to you. Dedicate a song to each child at your reception, or slip a special note under each child's place setting. Older children can greet guests, hand out programs, escort family members to their seats, and ask guests to sign your guest book or write notes to drop in a message bowl.

If your children aren't sitting with you, or if you have nieces and nephews who will be at your wedding, have a special kids' table at the reception. Older children may enjoy being given some responsibility. They can be in charge of their younger siblings or cousins and help keep them occupied. The children will love sitting together and feeling a sense of being on their own. You can cover the table with butcher paper so they can doodle, or provide little coloring books you design on your computer with drawings of you and your groom. You can save the drawings for your scrapbook. Ask them to create a cover for your wedding album. With such an important task, they may get so immersed you might not be able to drag them away.

> ## Second-Time Smarts
>
> Give each child a present either the night before or on the day of your wedding to let them know how special they are and to thank them for being part of the wedding.

Making Sure Your Children Don't Get Lost in the Shuffle

No matter how many times you tell your kids about what to expect at your wedding and how the evening will progress (remember, this may be their first wedding ever and weddings can be very over-whelming in general), it's still easy for your children to get lost in the shuffle as the day begins to take on a life of its own. You re-member how fast your first wedding went by. Don't get so caught up in the event that you leave your kids in the dust, sitting with Aunt Glenda in the back of the room, hoping your honeymoon flight will be cancelled.

Whether younger or older, your children may not be ready for you to get married. No matter how much you try to include them, they won't be excited. You can't let that stop you from enjoying your wedding. If they want to sulk, they will sulk with or without a ceremony.

Your children may be shy and not want to take on any roles that put them in the spotlight. That's fine. You may think they would look so cute walking down the aisle or singing a song at the reception, but don't force them to do something they aren't com-fortable doing. You don't need to be a stage mom at your wedding.

If you are worried about your little ones becoming fidgety or loud during the ceremony, have a backup game plan. When their moment arrives and they are frozen behind closed doors, hanging on the wedding coordinator's skirt crying and refusing to walk down the aisle, just roll with it. Kids are unpredictable. Even though they may have practiced walking down the aisle with you for months, they may become shy when it comes to the real thing.

Have grandparents or special friends wait for them in the front row at the end of the aisle so they have someone to walk toward. Then they can sit down for the ceremony, and you don't have to worry about them having to stand up for a half hour.

It helps to have a schedule of activities for your children and to remind them of relatives and friends they will see at the wedding, says Diane Forden. You can also spend some quality time with them while you and your groom are apart. "Make a fuss over your children while their hair is getting done, share a morning breakfast, and let them sit with you while you are getting ready," says Diane. She also recommends having a close family member watch them so you can dance with your new husband without your children clinging to you all night. "At some point you need to have your child go with someone else so you can spend time with your husband."

Finding Little Clothes

If you have teenagers, and your wedding is formal, they can wear what the wedding party is wearing—gowns and tuxedos. If you need to find fancy attire for your little ones, there are plenty of companies offering elegant evening wear for kids.

Flower girl dresses have come a long way. How could they not, with designers like Vera Wang getting into the act? You no longer have to watch your child turn into a puffball of white tulle and pink sashes. Designers today realize that a simpler dress can still look feminine and youthful.

Recent looks splashing the kids' fashion pages include designs that are far from babyish. You may be tempted to ask, "Do you have that in my size?" I'm not kidding. How about a raspberry silk taffeta tank dress or a pink silk shantung top and skirt or a lavender silk halter dress? Imagine your little guy in a single- or double-breasted gabardine suit, or a little Eton suit.

In my research I came across many sites that offer special-occasion clothing for children. Here is a sampling:

- www.theperfectpear.com
- www.isabelgarreton.com
- www.rosettamillington.com
- www.joancalabrese.net

Though you don't have to wrap your daughter in head-to-toe ruffles, do not dress her in something too mature or racy. She doesn't need a strapless gown even if the bridesmaids are wearing them. She also doesn't need to wear anything black or skin-tight.

As picture-perfect as you want your kids to be, it's more important that their clothes are comfortable, or you'll never hear the end of it. Make sure the material doesn't scratch their skin and that it doesn't make them sweat. Be sure they wear comfortable shoes. If you buy new shoes for the event, have them break them in before your wedding.

Shopping for those special outfits may be more fun than shopping for your gown. Your heart melts every time you see your son trying on little tuxes and your daughter modeling her precious flower girl dress. Your children will amaze you and help make your wedding day one of the greatest days of your life. Don't be surprised if they're already showering the bride with tons of hugs and kisses!

Yikes, This Is It!

FINAL PREPARATION FOR THE BIG DAY AND BEYOND

Here's where you start finalizing all the musts! I've provided a list to help you along:

• A couple of days before your wedding get on the horn to follow up with all your vendors. Verify that they know where to be, and when. You don't want any no-shows due to forgetfulness or mistakes in booking. Finalize arrangements, give the caterer the final guest number, and schedule a time to pick up your gown.

• Treat yourself—hire a cleaning service so you don't have to worry about staying on top of laundry and mopping the week or two before your wedding.

• Drink plenty of water.

• Go to bed early. This is not the week to start pulling all-nighters.

• Order takeout. You don't need to bother with grocery shopping when chances are you're going out of town for a week or more on your honeymoon.

• Exercise. Ideally, you found time for exercise throughout your engagement. Whether you kickbox, twist into a pretzel, bike ride, step, stomp, run, walk, swim, or spin, exercise throughout your engagement and the day before or day of your wedding to release stress.

Wedding Day Do's

• Get your fix! The day of your wedding is *not* the day to skip your morning coffee if you are used to drinking it every day. You don't want to be irritable or start getting a headache on your big day. Save withdrawal for another time.

• Allow plenty of time for primping so you can get your hair and makeup done at a leisurely pace and not feel that the artist is smearing colors on your face in order to get you in front of the camera in 10 minutes.

• Wear a button, snap, or zipper shirt so you don't have to risk ruining your makeup or hair when you need to change into your dress.

• Eat. This is a must. You want your energy so you won't be a grumpy bride. Don't use nerves as an excuse. One bride who didn't eat started throwing up the minute she had a sip of wine at her reception. Ask your wedding coordinator to set up some snacks. Just don't indulge in barbeque potato chips, cheese curls, cranberry juice, or anything else that could leave orange or red marks on your gown. Choose crackers, clear soft drinks, water, granola bars, and not-too-juicy fruit.

Practice Makes Perfect

If your wedding party is small, you don't necessarily need a rehearsal. If your children will be your attendants, you can practice on your own at home. But if you are having a larger group participating in the ceremony, a rehearsal can make for a stress-free wedding day. Everyone involved will know their places, what their cue is, and who walks in and out before them. You'll want your attendants, children, parents, and anyone else participating in the ceremony to be at the rehearsal. If two of your bridesmaids can't make it because their flight doesn't get in until later, don't worry. Carry on with the rehearsal. The wedding coordinator or another bridesmaid will fill them in before the wedding. Don't take this role on yourself—you've got enough to do.

Ideally, you want to rehearse in the actual ceremony room. It helps to know exactly where you will be standing in the church, temple, hotel, or restaurant, and how long the aisle will be. But often it's not possible to book the room because it's being used for another wedding or event. You may be able to arrange for a rehearsal earlier in the day. It's a good idea to have the rehearsal the day before your wedding so any out-of-town ceremony participants can make it.

If you can't get the wedding location, you can hold a rehearsal pretty much anywhere. You can invite everyone to your house or meet in a park to practice walking and placement of the bridesmaids and groomsmen. It helps to have a wedding coordinator to direct people and quiet everyone down. You don't want to be the bossy bride orchestrating your own rehearsal. Leave the job to someone else unless you and your groom really want to run it together in a low-key kind of way. However, I find with large wedding parties (grandparents, ringbearers, groomsmen, bridesmaids, flower girls, parents of the bride, parents of the groom, all walking down the aisle or giving readings), the rehearsal can get very disorganized. Trust me, you'll just want to socialize with your nearest and dearest.

Wedding Day Reflections

Take time out with your fiancé in the days leading up to the wedding. The best thing we did was spend a week together in Florida prior to our wedding. We were able to relax and reconnect and forget the wedding planning stress.

—Jessica

The rehearsal dinner is a nice time to get your out-of-towners, wedding party, and immediate family together for a relaxed night before your wedding. You can introduce people who have never met and enjoy your friends' company without being dressed up and worrying that it's all being videotaped. Some couples say the rehearsal dinner is more fun than the wedding. It's more intimate, and people are drinking and probably giving funny and heartfelt toasts to you and your groom. You can hold the dinner anywhere, from your house to your favorite bistro. It's up to you. Traditionally, the groom's parents pay for it and plan it, or you and your groom may pay for the whole weekend yourselves. Usually, the people who pay do the planning. If you feel too overwhelmed to plan the rehearsal dinner, you can trust the job to your groom.

Should We Shack Up the Night Before?

If you want to spend the night sleeping in your groom's arms, or spooning with him, or just hearing him snore beside you, I'm not going to tell anyone. You may not be able to sleep well at your parents' house in your old bed anyway. If the familiar works, don't rock the boat. You want to get a good night's sleep before your wedding.

Speaking of sleep, I know from experience that a main ingredient of a stress-free wedding day is feeling rested and refreshed. I had insomnia the night before my first wedding. Needless to say, I was a bit crabby in the makeup chair the next morning. Not willing to leave sleep to chance, I took a mild sleeping pill the night before my second wedding, and I slept like a baby.

Make a List and Check It Twice

Decide with your groom who will be responsible for bringing what to the wedding.

- Marriage license.
- Rings.
- Contact numbers for all your vendors.
- Your identification.
- Your gown, shoes, and accessories.
- Your children and their clothing.
- Your overnight bags (complete with any necessities such as prescription medication, contacts, or glasses).
- Your cell phone.
- Paper and pen (in case you have to jot down some last-minute words of thanks).
- Cash and envelopes for tips to vendors.

The Bride's Bag

I talked to brides, makeup artists, hairstylists, wedding coordinators, mothers of the brides, and others to find out what to include in the bride's bag. Obviously, you can't stuff everything into your little beaded vintage bag, but you can make sure your wedding coordinator or Mom has a toiletry case of goods set aside that you can get to before and after the ceremony.

Bridal Bag
Lipstick
Waterproof mascara
Breath mints
Face-blotting tissues
Brush
Comb
Baby powder
Hairspray
Clear nail polish
Cotton swabs
Ibuprofen
Safety pins
Scissors
Needle and white thread
White tape
Emery board
Tampons or pads
Bug spray
Umbrella
Quick-bonding glue (one bride glued her earring back together)
Clothes steamer
Tissue\
Toothbrush and Toothpaste

Working the Room

You are going to want to make the rounds of your guest tables. Surely, your friends and family will want to hug you and tell you that you are the most gorgeous bride they've ever seen. It's fun to see everyone you love in one room, but there isn't enough time to get into a conversation with everyone. You know how the night flies by. Just grab your husband's hand and make a sweep around the room smiling, saying hello, and moving on the next person, quickly. And be careful if you leave alone for the ladies' room. You may get cornered by Uncle Joe, who wants to talk to you and share stories of funny things you did when you were little. That's great, but not on your wedding night. You don't have 20 minutes to give each guest. Heck, in a four-hour reception with roughly 150 guests you don't have five minutes to give every guest.

Once you make your rounds you can eat your dinner and then dance all night. You might want to make a little pact with your groom not to get dragged off to opposite sides of the room by friends or relatives. This is your night. Hold hands, dance together, and revel in the joy of your wedding.

Looking Ahead

I asked relationship experts to offer advice on how to prepare for the first year of marriage and beyond:

"Getting through the first year of marriage can be tough, especially when you are becoming a stepparent. Children, particularly teenagers, can make you feel very inadequate as a stepparent. Don't take this personally. They do the same thing to their natural parents."

—DR. ROGER COLEMAN, PRESIDENT OF
CLERGY SERVICES, INC.

"Sometimes when couples get comfortable in a relationship, there is less passion. If things become routine, couples can get bored. The mad passion you feel in the beginning of a relationship should be replaced by warm

affection. Boredom can be overcome by varying your routine, for example, have sex in the living room or in the middle of the day."

—CHARLES T. HILL, PH.D., RELATIONSHIP EXPERT AND PROFESSOR OF
PSYCHOLOGY AT WHITTIER COLLEGE IN WHITTIER, CALIFORNIA

"Always romance one another. You can express yourself in your relationship with time, money, or creativity. Time and money are limited. Creativity is unlimited. For example, instead of buying him a card, leave him a CD of his favorite band on the counter with a note that says, for example, 'play song #7 to hear my message to you.' Or, do something nice for him that has to do with his hobbies. Does he collect baseball cards, photographs, wood airplanes, or wine?"

—GREG GODEK, AUTHOR OF *1,001 WAYS TO BE ROMANTIC*

Secrets for Marriage Success

Some couples say that a happy marriage can come down to a few basics: separate tubes of toothpaste and a king-size bed. But what works for one couple may not work for another. Here are some real women's secrets for keeping the marriage strong:

"It's easy to get caught up in the daily hustle and bustle of life and lose sight of what's most important: your family and your partner. Little things you do each day can help remind both of you of how important you are to each other. We start each day with 'I love you.'"

—LISA

"Be friends, be lovers, and learn the art of compromise. Have a sense of humor and be able to admit when you are wrong."

—JACKIE

"Learn from the past but don't dwell in the past. Start fresh, communicate, be honest, and be true to yourself."

—MISSY

"We have a date night every Saturday night, but we also take time to ourselves. I let him watch all his football games and he lets me shop or do whatever I want to do. Everyone needs their little things that they do by themselves. We've been married 13 years."

—SUSAN

"We talk through everything and we keep separate checking accounts."

—BECKY

"I always tell my husband how much I appreciate his buying the groceries and he'll thank me for clearing up the dishes. We don't take each other for granted."

—KATY

"We have 'his' and 'hers' everything, from cars to bank accounts and hobbies. Remind yourself of how far you've come."

—NORA

"If any old 'baggage' comes up from the past, talk it through. Our secret is simple: laughter, communication, romance, sports, and date nights."

—SUZY

"Be unconditionally loving and accepting. Learn to let the little things go. Constantly tell your husband how much you love him. He'll do the same for you, and it makes for a very nice life."

—DIANNE

"Don't go to bed mad at each other. Most likely whatever you argue about is usually pretty insignificant in the grand scheme of things. As long as you both have your health, you can get through anything together."

—MICHELE

A Note from the Author

We live in a time when the phrase "life is short" has new meaning. Don't wait around and let love pass you by. If you are deliriously happy but worry how your friends, relatives, or community will react to your getting married again, do something crazy: Put yourself first. Go ahead and spend your life with the person you love. Enjoy your magnificent wedding and grow old together. Remember, second chances are sweet, and dreams do come true.

Remember to smile, laugh, sing, dance, kiss, hope, hug, and dream at your wedding and beyond. Enjoy this special time. May your wedding be wonderful and your romance endless. Congratulations!

Resources

Wedding-Related Resources on the Web

Here are some Web sites that may help you get started with your planning.

Hiring Vendors

American Disc Jockey Association (www.adja.org)

American Institute of Floral Designers (www.aifd.org)

American Rental Association (www.rentalHQ.com)

Association of Bridal Consultants (www.bridalassn.com)

International Special Events Society (www.ISES.com)

Leading Caterers of America (www.leadingcaterers.com)

The National Association of Catering Executives (www.nace.net)

National Bridal Service (www.nationalbridalservice.com)

Professional Photographers of America (www.ppa.com)

Second Weddings Showcase (www.secondweddingshowcase.com)

Society of American Florists (www.aboutflowers.com)

Wedding and Event Videographers Association (www.weva.com)

www.booklivemusic.com

www.proDJ.com

Good to Know

California Cut Flower Commission (www.ccfc.org)

International Formalwear Association (www.formalwear.org)

International Freeze-Dry Floral Association (www.ifdfa.com)

Sigma Custom Wedding Maps (www.sigmamaps.com)

Stepfamily Association of America (www.saafamilies.org)

United States Post Office (www.usps.com)

www.betterbusinessbureau.com

www.chamberofcommerce.com

www.cocktail.com

www.ebay.com

www.familymedallion.com

www.lawyers.com

www.mapquest.com

www.regalrents.com

www.youngwidowsandwidowers.com

Wedding Planning Information

www.africanweddingguide.com

www.theknot.com

www.thepartygoddess.com

www.todaysbride.com

www.twiceisnicebride.com

www.weddingchannel.com

www.weddinggazette.com

www.weddingthemes.com

www.wedplan.com

Attire

After Six (www.aftersix.com)

Amsale (www.amsale.com)

Amy Michelson (www.amymichelson.com)

Carolina Herrera (www.carolinaherrerabridal.com)

David's Bridal (www.davidsbridal.com)
Haberman Fabrics (www.habermanfabrics.com)
Lazaro (www.lazarobridal.com)
Liz Lange (www.lizlange.com)
Michelle Roth (www.michelleroth.com)
Monique Lhuillier (www.moniquelhuillier.com)
Nicole Miller (www.nicolemiller.com)
The Paper Bag Princess (www.thepaperbagprincess.com)
Serafina (www.serafina.net)
Vera Wang (www.verawang.com)
Vintage Vixen (www.vintagevixen.com)
Watters and Watters (www.watters.com)
www.BridesMade.com
www.bridesmaids.com

Children's Clothing
www.bellakids.com
www.isabelgarreton.com
www.rosettamillington.com
www.theperfectpear.com

Accessories, Headwear, Shoes, Lingerie
www.barenecessities.com
www.biggerbras.com
www.bridaljewelryoutlet.com
www.bridalshoes.com
www.designershoes.com
www.eveningbags.com
www.heavenlyheadpieces.com
www.homabridal.com
www.kennethcole.com
www.lingerie4brides.com
www.myglassslipper.com

www.perfectdetails.com

www.stuartweitzman.com

www.TammyDarling.com

www.victoriassecret.com

www.wintersandrain.com

www.wonderbra.com

Beauty and Makeup

Bobbi Brown Professional Cosmetics
     (www.bobbibrowncosmetics.com)

Clinique (www.clinique.com)

Laura Mercier (www.lauramercier.com)

LORAC Cosmetics (www.loraccosmetics.com)

MAC Cosmetics (www.maccosmetics.com)

Max Factor (www.maxfactor.com)

Maybelline (www.maybelline.com)

Paula Dorf Cosmetics (www.pauladorf.com)

Revlon (www.revlon.com)

Sephora (www.sephora.com)

Stila Cosmetics (www.stilacosmetics.com)

Invitations, Programs, and Other Paper Keepsakes

Anna Griffin Invitation Design (www.annagriffin.com)

Crane's (www.crane.com)

Julie Holcomb Printers (www.julieholcombprinters.com)

www.atthepage.com

www.ChelseaPaper.com

www.makingmemorieslast.com

www.michaels.com

www.paperstyle.com

www.petalsnink.com

www.scrapbookingwithus.com

Registering

Barneys (www.barneys.com)

Bed Bath & Beyond (www.bedbathandbeyond.com)

Bloomingdales (www.bloomingdales.com)

Crate & Barrel (www.crateandbarrel.com)

Eddie Bauer Home Store (www.eddiebauer.com)

Fortunoff (www.fortunoff.com)

The Home Depot (www.homedepot.com)

Macy's (www.macys.com)

MarriedForGood.com (www.marriedforgood.com)

Neiman Marcus (www.neimanmarcus.com)

Pier One Imports (www.pierone.com)

Pottery Barn (www.potterybarn.com)

REI (www.rei.com)

Restoration Hardware (www.restorationhardware.com)

Sears (www.sears.com)

Smith & Hawken (www.smithandhawken.com)

Target (www.target.com)

Tiffany & Co. (www.tiffany.com)

TripChest.com (www.tripchest.com)

Williams-Sonoma (www.williams-sonoma.com)

www.giveforchange.com

www.Redenvelope.com

www.thehoneymoon.com

www.wine.com

www.winemonthclub.com

www.yourhoneymoonregistry.com

Magazines

Bridal Guide (www.bridalguide.com)

Bride Again (www.brideagain.com)

Bride's Magazine (www.brides.com)

Elegant Bride (www.elegantbride.com)

In Style Weddings (www.instyle.com)

Modern Bride (www.modernbride.com)

Premier Bride (www.premierbride.com)

Southern Bride (www.southernbride.com)

Southern Living Weddings (www.SouthernProgress.com
　　/southernliving/weddings/)

Wedding Bells (www.weddingbells.com)

Wedding Dresses Magazine (www.weddingdresses.com)

Wedding Pages (www.weddingpages.com)

Index

S

About the Author

PHOTO BY PAUL KUBEK

Julie Weingarden Dubin, a full-time freelance writer and a second-time bride, has covered a broad range of topics ranging from breast cancer and binge drinking to infertility and teen popularity. Her subject specialties include relationships, health, parenting, psychology, business, women, weddings, and pop culture.

A national magazine journalist, Julie has written for *Bridal Guide*, *Newsweek*, *Cosmopolitan*, *Good Housekeeping*, *Marie Claire*, *Redbook*, *Reader's Digest*, *Ladies' Home Journal*, *Psychology Today*, *Parenting*, *Woman's Day*, *First for Women*, *American Baby*, *Adweek*, *Seventeen,* and *Teen*.

Julie is a member of the American Society of Journalists and Authors, and she received her journalism degree from the University of Wisconsin, Madison. Julie lives in Huntington Woods, Michigan, with her husband, Bobby; son, Joshua; and golden retriever, Emma Lou.

Contact Julie via e-mail (JulieDubin@aol.com) to share your wedding story or to order signed copies of this book.